Answering the Call of the Wild

To Pam
Cathryn

Answering
the Call of the Wild

The Remarkable Life of Cathryn Hosea Hilker

Kathryn E. Merchant

Kathy Merchant (signature)

ORANGE *frazer* PRESS
Wilmington, Ohio

Published for the copyright holder by:
Orange Frazer Press
37½ West Main St.
P.O. Box 214
Wilmington, OH 45177

For price and shipping information, call: 937.382.3196
Or visit: www.orangefrazer.com

Book and cover design by:
Kelly Schutte and Orange Frazer Press

Library of Congress Control Number: 2021905087

First Printing

Printed in the United States of America

Sponsors

With sincere gratitude for gifts to the Cincinnati Zoo to sponsor Cathryn Hilker's biography, we thank you for helping to bring this book to life.

We especially want to thank the following generous sponsors for their early leadership gifts: Craig Maier; Karen Maier and the KFM Fund of Greater Cincinnati Foundation; Phil and Julie Myers and The Philip R. Myers Family Foundation; and Bobbie Unnewehr and The Marge & Charles J. Schott Foundation.

Cathryn's friends and family supporters include Helen Andrews, Dr. Diane Babcock, Trudi Fullen, Carl and Alice Hilker, Cathy Jacob, Carl and Kris Kalnow, Dr. Cora Ogle, and Dr. Nancy Zimpher.

By underwriting the cost of developing Cathryn's biography, these generous donors have helped to ensure that book sales will benefit The Angel Fund and future cheetah conservation initiatives.

—Thane Maynard, Zoo Director

Table of Contents

Preface

Beyond any doubt, we as humans love animals.
Whether we know it or not, somewhere in our hearts, somewhere in our past history,
we were part of the animal world.

I confess that I did not want to be the focus of a book. Many people have asked me to write my autobiography, but I honestly didn't see why my story might be interesting. There are so many accomplished and wonderful people who have influenced the course of my life. Now *that* is interesting. Any book about my life should be their stories.

My beloved cheetahs are the centerpiece of my life. I was fascinated by them, from first sightings as a young child at the Cincinnati Zoo to the privilege of raising them on my farm and being their trainer for the Cat Ambassador Program. Along with my horses, they are the long thread of who I am, of my soul, from the time I was a little girl until this moment at age 89. My story should be about the cats—Angel, Sarah, Kenya, Moya and my wonderful mountain lion, Carrie Cougar.

About seven years ago, I capitulated to friendly pressure and started writing an autobiography. I didn't get much further than a pair of stories about my early years on our family's Mason farm. So in this crazy year of 2020, I finally agreed to let someone else write my story, but with firm conditions about focusing on people and cats.

This book is dedicated to my son Carl. While horses and big cats were not his favorite "friends," he put up with them with good will. Note: we all survived.

I am grateful to the people who encouraged me to participate in this book, and who created a warm and thoughtful environment to meander through the

Nancy Zimpher, Kris Kalnow, Cora Ogle, and Cathryn Hilker. Cincinnati Country Club, August 7, 2020.

stories of my past (as well as an old musty trunk of memorabilia!). Thanks especially to Cora Ogle, Nancy Zimpher, and Kris Kalnow, who got the ball rolling and supported the whole process.

Thank you to Thane Maynard for everything you have done with and for me, and to the Cincinnati Zoo for sponsoring this book. I am thrilled to be able to continue helping to support cheetah conservation by sharing my story.

My special thanks go to Kathy Merchant, who did so much research to flesh out this story and tie together so many loose ends, and for hearing my wish that this book be a reflective pool of the people and cheetahs who anchor my life.

—*Cathryn Hosea Hilker*

Author's Note

Cathryn Hosea made a brash decision in 1957, when she was just 26, to spend two months in Africa with a man she barely knew. It was love at first sight. You may be thinking that this encounter led to a trip down the aisle. No, quite the contrary. Cathryn was single until she married Carl "Hege" Hilker, Jr., in 1969 when she was nearly 38. On that fateful trip, Cathryn fell in love with Africa in the shadow of Mt. Kilimanjaro and found an enduring passion for cheetahs in the wild that exploded into action when a cheetah named Angel entered her life.

If Cathryn had her way, her entire life story would be told in the frame of big cats. And if pressed, she would admit that she likes (and relates to) animals better than people. To be fair, this book partially honors Cathryn's wish for a cat-centric story. But leaving out the many other parts of her story—the long trail of horses running through her life, how she got to Africa in 1957 and so many times after that, what happens when you won't take "no" for an answer, or when your answer was "no" when it should have been "yes," and the fantastic mix of people who shaped her life and career—would be to miss the essence of a very accomplished woman.

Cathryn Hosea Hilker's "second act" began a half-life ago when she was about 43. Initially as a volunteer at the Cincinnati Zoo & Botanical Garden, then as a part-time staffer just as she was turning 50 and Angel came into her life, Cathryn pioneered a Cat Ambassador Program that showcased the Zoo's cheetahs and big cats in schools and other venues offsite from the Zoo campus. She raised cougars, lions, and cheetahs on her farm in Mason, Ohio. With her husband Hege, Cathryn funded the purchase of a farm in Namibia devoted to cheetah conservation. In her own version of "lions and tigers and bears, oh my!" Cathryn was the wizard of the Zoo's education stage, captivating generations of school children and their parents while dusting audiences with a few sprinkles of wildlife education.

Her unwavering love for these beautiful cats endures today as Cathryn prepares to celebrate her 90th birthday on June 22, 2021. This book honors her incredible life journey and will undoubtedly inspire all who read it to believe that anything is possible. Just do it!

This book is not strictly chronological. Rather, it is a series of memorable stories, intertwined, told by and about Cathryn, and by the people who have made a significant difference in her life.

As she describes it, "your life is defined by the people you meet." I couldn't agree more. Thank you, Cathryn, for the privilege of sharing your story in this book.

—*Kathy Merchant*

Answering the Call of the Wild

Cathryn Hilker (2005)

1

Beginnings

—◦◦◦—

*I was defined by growing up in a farm setting. It was my whole world as
a child. My best friends when I was very small were my three brothers,
my pony, my dog, my cat, and our farmer.* —*Cathryn Hilker*

Family life on a farm was the centerpiece of Cathryn's formative years,
supplying her childhood experiences and defining her character as an adult.
Like so many people of the "silent generation,"[1] she did not get to meet her
grandparents or great-grandparents, nor did she get to know many of her
aunts, uncles, or cousins. The tight bond she formed with her parents and
three siblings created a soft perimeter for a world full of love and opportunity. This cocoon gave Cathryn the freedom to roam unbridled through fields
and forests, to explore the life of the mind without restraint, and to unite the
spirit of her animals into her very being.

—◦◦◦ A Short Family Tree [2] ◦◦◦—

Cathryn Ann Hosea was born June 22, 1931, the fourth child and only
daughter of Frank Hoyt Hosea and Helen Ida Mastio Hosea. Though many of
Cathryn's ancestors hailed from states to the south of Ohio, she has lived in
the Cincinnati area her entire life.

In August 1919, when he was 27 years old, Frank Hosea met and married
Helen Mastio. Just shy of her 19th birthday when they married, Helen was a
beautiful, tall young woman from Warren County. Cathryn's three brothers
Harold, Frank, and Bob were born in quick succession—in 1921, 1923, and
1925 respectively. Cathryn came along six years later.

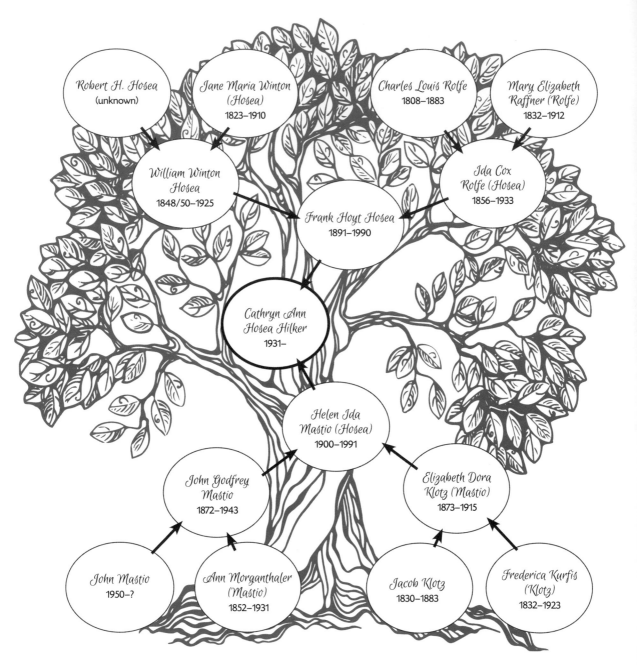

Helen's parents were John G. Mastio and Elizabeth Dora Klotz Mastio. Cathryn never met her maternal grandmother because Elizabeth died in 1915 when Helen was only 14 years old. She never met her maternal grandfather either because he was estranged from the family. By marrying Frank, Helen had escaped an abusive father and gained a husband who was, according to Cathryn's telling of this family story, "a mature, established gentleman who treated her with kindness and respect."

Grandmother Mastio had two older sisters who never married, Catherine ("Katie") and Anna Klotz. These sisters, who were born about a year apart (around 1865 and 1866), were Cathryn's great aunts. They lived with the Hoseas and figured prominently in Cathryn's early family story. Named Cathryn Ann, she is their namesake.

Frank Hosea's family roots trace back to Kentucky, Virginia, and West Virginia, but he was born and spent most of his life in Ohio. His parents, William Winton Hosea and Ida Cox Rolfe (Hosea), presumably met in West Virginia. It is where Ida's mother grew up and where William and Ida married in 1875.

Family lore suggests that William Hosea lost the family's Virginia farm homestead at the end of the Reconstruction Era (1865–77) following the Civil War, and then shuttled back and forth between Virginia, West Virginia, and Ohio until his death in 1925. (It is possible that the Virginia farm actually belonged to Cathryn's grandmother, or more generally to the Rolfe family. Ida's father, Charles Louis Rolfe, was born and raised in Mecklenberg, Virginia.)

Five of Frank's seven siblings were born in Ohio, one in Virginia, another in West Virginia. Cathryn's father was sixth in line (1891). Grandfather Hosea died before Cathryn was born, and though Grandmother Hosea lived until 1933, Cathryn was too young to remember her.

At age 82, Cathryn Hosea Hilker started writing the foundational stories for a memoir about her family and their farm. These stories illuminate how Cathryn's earliest days on her family's farm in Mason, Ohio, shaped her life as an adult and moved her deeply to become an iconic wildlife conservationist.

With Cathryn's permission, now at age 89, these excerpts in quotation marks offer personal imprints in her own words.

—∞ The Hosea Family ∞—

My parents were marvelous people, and I idolized them both. —Cathryn Hilker

"The most important influence on my life was my father, Frank Hosea. I absorbed his drive and determination, his love of the land, and also his impatience when progress came too slowly. My father worked from the time he was a young teenager and, in one of his lifelong regrets, he was not able to finish high school.

The experience left him with determination—and I heard this my whole life—that he was not going to raise his children the way he had been raised. He was not going to force his children to go to work too soon. They were going to go to school, they were going to go to college, and they were going to have a far better life then he had ever known. Looking back now, I see that he was defined by place and work coupled with the will to excel and succeed."

Frank Hosea (r) wears cement mud (circa 1949)

Frank's first job in the construction industry created the pathway to his success in business. He drove a team of mules pulling a heavy iron blade that would clear construction sites and level the land. It was slow work and very physical. Cathryn's image of her father's first job from the stories he would tell is that the construction methods of that era weren't "as primitive as the building of the pyramids, but it might have come close. A bulldozer was far from anyone's imagination."

Frank Hosea worked for a construction company for several years, gaining seniority and a team of workers. His job paid $10 a week, a handsome sum in those days, increasingly important with a wife and young son. An insight into the source of Cathryn's personality and determination is revealed in this story from about 1930 as it has been handed down over the years:

In what I believe was the turning point of his life, my father had a disagreement with a man for whom he worked. He was called into the office and summarily fired. My father said that he left the room and slammed the door so hard that the glass shattered. He never looked back. But then he had to go home and tell my mother. She was scared to death that he would never get a job that paid him that much again.

He first borrowed money from my mother's two maiden aunts, Anna and Katie Klotz, who sold some stock they owned in what was then the American Rolling Mill Company (a rolled steel manufacturer known today as the AK Steel Corporation). It was enough money for Dad to start his own construction company. He bought a cement mixer, several shovels, a hammer, a scraper, and a sander that he used while on his hands and knees to put smooth finishing touches on cement.

He secured what was then a huge contract with the City of Cincinnati, making several hundred dollars to build some of the city's first sidewalks. It was hard labor. It was the beginning of a respectable, successful business called the H & FH Hosea Company[3] which eventually, when my brothers took over the company, built all of the bridges on Interstate 71 from Cincinnati to Columbus.

Cathryn's father started his own company during the depression and made most of his living pouring sidewalks for people living in suburban Hyde Park and Indian Hill. "I heard so many stories about how hard he worked with only one helper and a cement mixer. He basically didn't trust anyone else to

🐾 Frank and Helen Hosea at the Golden Lamb (1980s)

do the work correctly. My mother said he always came home with his hands, trousers, and shoes full of cement. Mother would say 'Frank, why do you wear those good clothes? You can't send cement to the dry cleaners.'"

Cathryn remembers distinctly a long list of principles that she says were "drummed into us relentlessly. Always take care of yourself. Never lie. Do not cheat. Be honest. Do not do things that people will hold against you. Don't ever give up. There is no such thing as can't. Stand up straight. Put your shoulders back. Take care of your body. Don't drink. Don't smoke. Don't throw yourself away." Words to live by, as Cathryn describes them: "timeless tenets of morality and clean living." These life rules clearly penetrated and stuck. They are threaded throughout decisions Cathryn made during the rest of her life.

"While it was my father's passion and determination that shaped me, my mother was nevertheless an ever-present force. She was utterly dependable, always there for us when Dad was at work. She was the binding strength that kept everyone together, including my father. Seldom prone to anger, she was the most wonderful, soothing force in my life, and utterly supportive of everything I did. It seemed to me that she could do everything, without ever

Answering the Call of the Wild
The Remarkable Life of Cathryn Hosea Hilker

appearing to be rushed, even when my brothers were running in three different directions. Like my father, she was strong, disciplined, and consistent."

Helen Hosea took care of her husband's office administration, writing checks, paying taxes, whatever it took. The two live-in maiden aunts took care of the family's domestic duties. Cathryn was free to roam the farm and ride horses to her heart's content. Years later, Cathryn's mother tried to teach her bookkeeping. "She tried, bless her heart. She would have me read numbers to help her. If she made a mistake, I had to read the numbers back to her and she could find the error. But I wanted nothing to do with it. I wanted to be outside, to ride my pony. I was very resistant to the administrative work."

The Hoseas were a tall family. "My mother was about five-foot-seven or eight, and dad was six-foot-three. My brothers were all six-five. And I was six-two." Although the entire family was quite close-knit, Cathryn was naturally closest to the youngest son Bob. They were best friends, certainly as youngsters living on a farm, and throughout the rest of their lives. "I adored my brother Bob."

"When it was time for dinner in our formal dining room, my mother would ring a huge dinner bell because we were scattered all over our 175-acre farm. By the time we sat down at the dinner table, everyone needed to be freshened up. You couldn't be wearing your stable-hand or outdoor play clothes. You had to be clean, including your hands. My brother Bob always failed Dad's hand inspection. Time and time again, he would be sent from the table to wash up, only to return having failed to use any soap, and then back to the sink he would go."

—∞ *The Farm in Mason, Ohio* ∞—

*My life was the farm—the workers, farm horses, cattle, sheep,
and thousands of turkeys. It enveloped me, and I enveloped it. I couldn't
imagine growing up anywhere else, except on the land. I used to throw myself on the
ground and just breathe in the smell of the earth.* —Cathryn Hilker

Cathryn was raised from the day she was born on the 175-acre farm near Mason, Ohio, in Warren County. "I grew up in the house my father built. A country home, our house was lovely—it had tall pillars. It was not big, it was not richly appointed, but it was full of love."[4] Cathryn's father bought this farm the year she was born, dreaming of being a farmer, but knowing that he needed to pursue a different path to provide for his growing family. Owning a farm would have to do.

Before Mason became a dense suburb situated between the cities of Cincinnati and Dayton, the community consisted mostly of large farms ranging from 100 to 300 acres. The Hosea family farm was accessible only by gravel roads. Her parents, three brothers, two maiden great aunts, myriad farm animals, and some imaginary friends were the extent of Cathryn's family bubble during those early years.

"I had no real playmates except my three older brothers, so I created a world in which I lived with my dog, cat, pony, and the people who worked on our farm. The farm included a 10-acre woodland filled with walnut trees where I frequently sequestered myself with my wonderful make-believe playmates. I knew and loved every inch of that farm because I had walked it, ridden my pony over it. For the first few years of my life, the farm was who I was. I didn't exist outside of that farm. It was the absolute center of my life."

The farm was a deeply sensory experience for Cathryn as well as a source of safety and security. As she remembers particularly her pre-school years wandering freely around the farm, the smell and feel of the land are most vivid.

"My earliest memories begin under the lilac bush in our front yard. The sweet-smelling lilac bush was the size of a small dining room. This is where I learned to feel part of the earth. Venturing out from that small oasis, the woods became beloved to me, and when I stayed there, I knew I was wonderfully safe. Even as a little girl of four or five, this is where I wanted to live.

If the sight of the woods captivated me, it was the scents that burned deepest into my memory. The smell of the dampness of that woodland was like nothing else on the farm. Every field has its own unique odor, and this woodland was distinguished from all other places on the farm because it had never been tilled. It held a wonderful dampness that I loved when I flattened myself to the ground and drew breath. I loved lying on the ground. My mother would say, 'get up off the ground, Cathryn, you're going to catch pneumonia.' I heard that all my life."

"Under a Lilac Bush" by Cathryn Hilker[5]

So few folks today know or care that in the 1930s, when I was a child, farmers worked from dawn to dusk, planting, harvesting and, most of all, tending to and watching their crops. We lived on a farm and I considered myself a farmer all through childhood. My father was a businessman in the city, but I spent every moment I could following our farmer. He owned a pair of draft horses, a pair of mules, two sets of work clothes, and one suit that he wore every Sunday. He lived with his son who was 10 years older than I in a farmhouse up the lane from our house that my father had built for my mother.

I galloped on my first horse, held in my mother's arms. That continued for years until I could ride my own pony. It was my first experience in receiving companionship from the relationship with another species. Could that single experience have fixed within that small person the longing to be in the world of another species?

I may as well have been born inside a lilac bush, huddled in among the roots and branches. The huge purple blossoms filling both hands, I felt such safety. I would not just smell the flowers. I would take in my entire breath, inhaling that sweet aroma. A full breath nearly made me dizzy. This is where I came on many summer days as a small child. If my three brothers tormented me or, even worse, told me that "I was a girl and had to stay home," I retreated to the huge lilac bush in our front yard. If I complained to my mother about any injustice I faced, she would dismiss them and remind me that there were a lot of activities for me.

I would find solace in my lilac bush.

I went back to my lilac today, 70 years later (on 3-31-2012). I returned to the pond, the warm, shallow water now turned to ice. The wild ducks who had spent the summer were gone now, the little holes of water they had diligently kept open, now frozen over. The big bull frogs, silent now, lying safely in the mud under the ice, waiting for spring. It was not a big pond, but it lies in the middle of the farm fields, fenced off from the cows who came to drink from a larger pond near the big cattle barns. I can see the edge of the ice pushing against the rim of the pond. I see some grains of whole corn, left there to feed the few remaining ducks as they valiantly tried to keep the hole open for swimming. They do seem to know when they are coming too close to danger, too close to the racoon or fox.

In the forest, the walnut trees and their companion shagbark hickory trees became Cathryn's first teachers, fueling her curiosity about the world and how it works. "The woods gave me life, defined who I was. I wanted to be there by myself, and I learned there by myself. As a child, I would tug at those long, wide strips of bark, lifting them up to see how they were attached and discovering the shagged layers beneath. In the fall, the walnut trees dropped their large, sweet nuts to the ground, which I stuffed in my pockets for an eventual forest feast of my own."

Frank Hosea was Cathryn's second teacher, deepening her connection with the earth and nature. They walked the farm together, climbing gates and fences through the pasture and into the woods. While Frank had not planted the walnut trees himself, he treated them like "arboreal children."

Our purposes on these walks differed. My father came to check on his prized walnut trees, while I came for discovery. I had no idea that walnut lumber was valuable, that trees could be cut down and sold. So on these walks, his purpose, and by delegation mine, was to chart how much the trees had grown. We did this every three or four months.

As Dad moved methodically toward the woods, I dawdled, spellbound by nature, searching for footprints or other evidence of living things near a little creek that ran through the pasture. One of my favorite pastimes was to get down on my hands and knees and watch the dung beetles burrow into the earth. I thought it was fascinating, and of course it drove my Dad out of his mind. If I dawdled to watch this process, he would warn me that he would come without me next time, so I would put my curiosity on hold and make an effort to keep up with him.

My father knew exactly which tree was where because he had a little map, and each tree had an identification number. He kept a record of each tree's circumference, moving efficiently from tree to tree. He would do the measuring, and I recorded the data in a small notebook.

Although Cathryn didn't know it at the time, the magic of the farm and her fascination with animals were harbingers of many things to come.

At night, with Mason the nearest town a mile away, there were no lights on the horizon, no ambient light from urban sprawl. We could look up and see the Milky Way, a glorious swath of starlight that invited contemplation of the universe and one's existence in it. After my young adulthood, I would never see the Milky Way like that again until I went to Namibia.

In nearby Mason were people I saw once a week. My mother imported young girls about my age because she wanted me to have friends. I was happy to see the girls but even happier when they left. I knew early on that we were different. They did things I didn't want to do. They brought their dolls, and they wanted to play dress-up. The closest I came to playing dolls was to dress up my 'little cheetah,' a big fuzzy cat named Fluffy, of all things! All the clothes from my dolls were on my cat. She was the best dressed house cat in Mason, pushed around in my doll carriage or carried in my arms while I rode my pony. My imported friends wanted to ride my pony, and later my horse. But I had no interest in their lives, and they really had no interest in mine.

Although as a young child Cathryn was not permitted to handle any big farm equipment, she rode along while the earth was being plowed to prepare for planting, reveling in the sights and smells of the process.

"It all smelled so good. The initial plowing was one smell as the earth broke. And then breaking the clods apart was another wonderful smell. The farmer had to wait until the earth dried just enough. If he plowed too early, the earth was lumpy. Too late and it turned to dust. Our fields were always perfectly smooth. You could walk in the center of a row of corn and the soil around you would be completely smooth. We didn't have a baler. We farmed with horses, picking the hay up with a pitchfork and tossing it onto a wagon."

Reflecting on the power of that experience, Cathryn notes "I'm sure that's one reason I loved Africa so much. The land is so fragrant—the trees, the smell of the herds of animals, the grunting sounds of the wildebeest. Every sense is stimulated by the earth."

The Hosea family farm was eventually subdivided among the four children. By that time, the farm was surrounded by concrete and big suburban homes, by light pollution and noise. Cathryn realized "you cannot go back home again. It's not what you remember, what it was." As Cathryn prepared in later years to sell her share of the farm, she realized that the buyer was planning to clear-cut the land including the valuable walnut trees her father had tended so carefully. She decided "this could not happen. The woods were part of my life; clear-cutting them would be akin to cutting off my leg."

Instead, Cathryn donated the woods and its precious trees to the City of Mason in memory of her father. The 13-acre Frank Hosea Woods is the only preserve remaining in a city of more than 30,000 people. "The woods my father and I prized are more valuable than ever now because of their mere existence, a small but priceless oasis amidst a crowded suburban area."

—✺ Horses ✺—

I did not know as a child that the wind in my face on a galloping pony would lead me to love speed, and lead eventually to try to understand and ultimately to save the fastest animal on earth—the cheetah. I only knew that horses were my love, a devotion I still carry to this day. —Cathryn Hilker

Cathryn's first horse was a little spotted Shetland pony named Prince. She was just five years old. Cathryn's mother, whose own horse was named Juanita, taught her to ride. She did not use a saddle or bridle, instead riding bareback using a halter and two ropes for reins. As Cathryn remembers this early experience, "Prince would gallop, stop on a dime, put his head down, and throw me over his head. He did this every day." As a result of this daily practice, Cathryn learned to become a very good rider at an early age.

Every girl who has a horse must also have a kitty, right? Cathryn's kitty was named Fluffy. "I adored Fluffy, and I carried her with me everywhere, including on my daily horse rides." More important, though, was Cathryn's destination: going to "work" for their farmer, Jack Fleckenstein.

Cathryn had decided that she was part of the summer farm-worker team. She really did have two important jobs. Every morning she rode her pony to the barn, tied it to a tree, and marched off to her first job caring for the huge, handsome Percheron draft horses that pulled the farm's machinery—plows, mowers, cull-packers, harrows. Her duties included brushing the horses. After Farmer Fleckenstein had put on their harnesses, he would let Cathryn lead them out of the barn to a water trough.

I was this tiny thing leading this huge horse. I don't know why my mother let me do it. I mean their feet are like dinner plates! But they were very gentle with me, and I think my mother knew she could trust our farmer not to put me in harm's way.

No farm animal captured my heart more than our horses. I'm sure (the workers) saw this little girl trotting up and thought 'Here she comes again. Her father owns the farm, so we can't tell her to go home.' I remember squeezing into the horse stalls so closely that they would have squashed me if they had leaned on me. Their heads were tied to the stalls, and those big old heads would turn as far as the rope would allow to greet me with a soft, gentle nicker. I was always struck by the flaw in their manes: the large, rough area where the mane was either tangled or the hair had worn away. That's where the collar went, and it was the mark of their life. They worked six days a week, from dawn to dark. I also helped to throw on the heavy harnesses by pushing the collar up. I would smooth the mane down under the collar so it wouldn't suffer as much wear and tear.

Being paid 50 cents a day was big money in the 1930s! Cathryn's second job, when she was a bit older, was to carry drinking water during harvest to the men who worked on the half dozen farms along the Hosea's gravel road. These were local farmers who moved from farm to farm with whatever large piece of equipment was needed at the time. The equipment was too expensive for any one farmer to own all of it. But machines had begun to replace the work of horses, so the farming process worked much like an informal co-operative.

I pumped two big jugs full of icy-cold water from our well. I rode bareback, sitting behind those jugs placed where the saddle would ordinarily be. The fields were a blur of activity as I approached on my pony. I knew the farmers were glad to see me on these occasions.

They always had a kind word for me as I rode up with the precious water. At the end of the day, the farmer whose land was being worked would give me 50 cents.

The draft horses worked six days a week, and on Sunday they rested unshackled, frolicking and sleeping in the nearby pasture. Come Monday morning, they were lured back to the barn and the prospect of a six-day work week by 10 ears of corn per horse. Cathryn shares a life lesson from watching the rhythm of the horses moving from work, to rest, and back again:

> They deserved that free time. They needed to feel that soft ground beneath them. And that philosophy has held true for my big cats, my cheetahs, that must be allowed to get out and feel the ground beneath their feet. I am profoundly saddened that so many animals in captivity never, ever get to feel the earth. How can one live, how can any creature truly live, and not feel the earth?

Along the way, Cathryn developed a passion for fox hunting. Her dear friend and thoroughbred breeder Ruth Venable introduced her to fox hunting and field trials "which added another dimension to my life." She jumped anything and everything—through swamps, up and down the rolling hills of Kentucky, over wire fences. "I learned how to follow hounds in 'speed and drive' hunting. I learned how to listen to the hounds, how to tell which hound was the lead, and how to follow the lead." In 1962, she placed sixth in field jumping. "I was so thrilled you would have thought I won the whole thing." Cathryn became an active member of the Camargo Hunt Club and was elected to its board of directors in 2005.

Cathryn also learned dressage, a calmer sport than fox hunting. Her long-time friend Catherine (Cathy) B. Jacob grew up on a farm that abutted the Camargo Hunt Club. Also an accomplished horsewoman, Cathy has been active in the United States Dressage Foundation. The Catherine B. Jacob Schooling Show "Year End Program Award," given annually, is named for her.

Cathy Jacob tells this story of their friendship spanning 60 years, cemented by their love for horses:

In the 40s and early 50s, the Camargo Hunt riders hunted the Mitchell Farm area. It was common for the hunt to go through green trail gates that allowed you to stay mounted while opening and closing them. During that time, it was my job to patrol the fences on our farm to make sure all the gates were closed. Our Hereford cows were notorious for pushing through fences and going into a neighbor's corn or bean fields.

In 1960, when I was 13, I met Cathryn while I was patrolling the fence line on my pony along the back forty of my parents' Mitchell Farm near Loveland. She and her friend Helen Andrews were trail riding over some of the old Camargo Hunt property when they wandered onto Mitchell Farm. We spied each other as Cathryn and Helen were coming through a gate. When Cathryn asked where they were, I responded 'you're on my farm!' That day we explored the farm property's trails as we rode back to the farmhouse and barns. That was the beginning of our friendship.

In the early 1960s, several like-minded people created the Miami Valley Hunt on some land they owned. Cathryn had gone to school with Helen Sproat who was part of that horse show and hunting group. Cathryn always loved to ride show hunters and jump cross country. Her naturally elegant slender body and long legs were fluid with the horses as they jumped over fences.

When Cathryn and Hege were married in May 1969, Cathryn's artist friend Edie Schmidt made informal pen-and-ink invitations to their wedding. It showed a tall, elegant fox in her wedding dress—so appropriate for Cathryn. Four years later, I had the privilege to wear her elegant wedding dress. The only alteration was to shorten one inch in the waist. Always something borrowed!

Cathryn loved her cats so much. When Cathryn started working at the Cincinnati Zoo and Angel came into her life, the cheetah went everywhere with her, including hunts. For her birthday, I had a belt made with brass plates engraved with their names riveted onto the leather. She wore that belt every day while she worked at the Zoo.

🐾 Perfect "1930s Form" on High Hope

Cathryn's love for riding horses continued unabated until about a decade ago when she lost her sense of balance and it was no longer safe for her to ride for pleasure or competition.

Meet some of Cathryn's prized stable of horses:

"My first horse—after my little pony Prince—was a hand-me-over from my brother Frank when he left to go into military service in WWII." Tony was born on the Mason farm. The Hoseas couldn't afford to buy a horse at that time, so Cathryn's mother bred a trotter with her own American saddle horse mare. "Tony was a funny looking foal. It was a rather ridiculous mating. But I still loved that horse. He was struck by lightning; the bolt shot from his horseshoes right up through his legs. That was the first time I ever witnessed death."

Cathryn describes High Hope as "the horse of my life. He did dressage, fox hunting, and fence jumping at local hunter trials. He was a magnificent horse."

When Cathryn first saw High Hope in the 1970s, she almost declined the opportunity to buy him from Ruth Venable. "It was the biggest foal they had ever had on their farm. Big horses are often quite ugly when they are born. Nothing fits together. Their heads are too big for their bodies, their legs are scrawny and too long. Their withers or rumps are too high. It's like a terrible puzzle."

But at six-foot-two, Cathryn needed a tall horse. Venable offered to keep the horse for a year, inviting Cathryn to come back to make a final purchase decision—at double the price! "That's the horse you want, Ruthie said to me, because that horse is going to grow."

Apparently Venable was right. When Cathryn saw High Hope as a yearling, she gladly paid the higher price. As High Hope grew into a mature horse, "he could really gallop and jump. We had a wonderful time winning cross-country events. He wasn't the best fox hunter in the world, but he was keen and our movements were in harmony. I loved him to death."

In January 2005, Cathryn bought a horse named Calendron ("Cal") from Entrophy Farm near Chicago for $20,000, "the most I ever spent on anything, let alone a horse." The next year she bought her final horse, Kelso, who is still alive and boarded at the Camargo Hunt Club. Kelso was even taller than High Hope. "I was one of the only people who could even get on him because the stirrups were so high."

⸎ Cathryn's Early Introduction to Cheetahs ⸎

As a young child, Cathryn was lovingly attached to her horses. Her passion to ride for pleasure and competition continued to capture her heart—for more than 75 years—throughout her adult years. But then along came the cats. Cheetahs gracefully glided into the center frame of Cathryn's life over several decades until the moment when Angel arrived to occupy center stage in 1981. She became entirely enchanted with cheetahs, determined to help save this endangered species, and there was no looking back.

"Ever since I was a child, it's always been their eyes. I used to stand at the cheetah exhibit at the Cincinnati Zoo looking at their eyes. My parents would leave me there because I stayed so long. I just watched them: those

beautiful golden eyes, those slender long legs. The way they walk—like thoroughbreds—is unique to cheetahs among the big cats. I never in the world thought I would have one, and when I finally did, it was like someone gave me a missing piece of my life."

The cheetahs invaded her childhood dreams, perhaps spurred on by a fanciful oil lamp in her parents' home. The lamp sat on a table in the hallway of her parents' farmhouse. It was fully adorned with scenes from Egypt—near the pyramids, in small villages, in a desert oasis—and all the animals that would appear naturally in those scenes including camels, elephants, and lions. She was unnerved by a scene with two bounty hunters aiming guns at a large spotted cat leaping out from the tall-fringed grass. This scene haunted and worried her waking hours when she pretended that she was actually in this scene.

But in her nighttime dreams, it was all sweetness and light. She had the same dream over and over. She was in a cave, completely dark except for one bright light. There were many different cats, but the cheetah would walk by her, so close she could reach out and touch it. Cathryn was captivated by the dream and determined to reach out and touch live cheetahs.

Hillsdale High School Graduation (1949)

2

Laying the Groundwork for Greatness (1956–60)

—◦◦◦—

Though much is taken, much abides; and though
We are not now that strength which in old days
Moved earth and heaven, that which we are, we are,
One equal temper of heroic hearts,
Made weak by time and fate, but strong in will
To strive, to seek, to find, and not to yield.
—*Excerpt from "Ulysses" by Alfred Lord Tennyson, 1833*

◦◦◦ Hillsdale High School (now Seven Hills) ◦◦◦

"Had I not gone to Hillsdale for high school, I think my life would've been very different because you were really challenged at Hillsdale, as students are today." Hillsdale is now Seven Hills.

With a note of sadness in her voice, Cathryn remembers the moment at Hillsdale when she discovered that her early years of public education in the tiny Mason schools had been a poor foundation for the future. "I always got straight As and thought I was doing really well. Then I got to Hillsdale, only to find that my As became Cs and Ds. I wasn't prepared for that environment, especially in reading, writing, and vocabulary. My English teacher said that I was nearly illiterate."

Calling upon the depth of determination she learned from her father, Cathryn vowed to overcome that challenge. She bought a book called *30*

Days to a More Powerful Vocabulary—a concept that remains alive and well today—and pushed herself to conquer reading and writing. Soon she developed a lifelong love of reading, especially Shakespeare and poetry. "Going to Hillsdale gave me confidence and communications skills."

—❧ It Was Already Decided: She Would Go to College ❧—

Like many 18-year-olds, Cathryn Hosea left high school in 1949 without a clear picture of what she wanted to do next. She had four abiding loves: her family, the family farm, horses, and (by then) reading. Although none of these embedded passions shed clear light on an immediate pathway for Cathryn to follow on her journey to college, she was absolutely going to go. That was her father's prescription for all four Hosea children.

Cathryn attended three different schools during the five years she spent completing a college degree, ultimately graduating from the University of Cincinnati in 1954 with a degree in cultural anthropology.

Her first year was at Rollins College, a liberal arts school in Winter Park, Florida. Cathryn laments that "my grades were not good enough to get into an Eastern school, which is where all my Hillsdale classmates were headed. The entrance requirements at Rollins were more relaxed then than they are today." Cathryn left Rollins after her freshman year, realizing on reflection that she had essentially repeated her senior year at Hillsdale.

In 1950, Cathryn headed west to Colorado. When asked why, her response was simple and clear: "I wanted to go west, ride horses, and study journalism." She enrolled in the University of Colorado (CU) at Boulder. The University's 1951 yearbook lists Cathy Hosea as a sophomore in the Arts & Sciences department.[6] After a second year at CU, she was restless and decided to return to Cincinnati.

Back home, living on her parents' farm, Cathryn settled into a degree program in cultural anthropology at the University of Cincinnati (UC). She graduated from the College of Arts & Sciences in 1954 just before her 23rd birthday.

With no immediate plans in sight to use her college degree, she scratched an itch to travel. (A life-altering trip to Africa in 1957 wasn't yet even a glimmer in her eye.) She took a job with United Service Organizations, Inc.

SPONSORS

With sincere gratitude for gifts to the Cincinnati Zoo to sponsor Cathryn Hilker's biography, we thank you for helping to bring this book to life.

We especially want to thank the following generous sponsors for their early leadership gifts: Craig Maier; Karen Maier and the KFM Fund of Greater Cincinnati Foundation; Phil and Julie Myers and The Philip R. Myers Family Foundation; and Bobbie Unnewehr and The Marge & Charles J. Schott Foundation.

Cathryn's friends and family supporters include Helen Andrews, Dr. Diane Babcock, Agnes Boswell, Paula Comisar, Robert Edmiston, Trudi Fullen, Roger Grein, Carl and Alice Hilker, Anne Ilyinsky, Cathy Jacob, Carl and Kris Kalnow, Katie Lawrence (Willow Hill Foundation), Marian and Jack Leibold, Martha Lindner, Linda Maier, Geoffrey Meyers, Dr. Cora Ogle, Wym and Jan Portman, and Dr. Nancy Zimpher.

By underwriting the cost of developing Cathryn's biography, these generous donors have helped to ensure that book sales will benefit The Angel Fund and future cheetah conservation initiatives.

Thane Maynard, Zoo Director

The Colorado Rockies circa 1951

(USO) and headed off to Guam to provide entertainment for members of the U.S. Armed Forces stationed there as the Korean War was winding down.[7] It was a radically adventurous move for the farm girl from Mason, Ohio, whose only trips to that point had been in mainland United States.

The USO was set up to serve as a GI's home away from home, to boost the morale of servicemen and women. This mission captured Cathryn's sense of purpose and adventure, so off she went to lead a corps of women responsible for organizing and providing entertainment for the men who were stationed at Anderson Air Force base in Guam. It was Cathryn's first professional job. USO was best known for its live performances called camp shows. "I could play the piano, so I used to provide accompaniment for songfests for the service men, and I organized all the lunches and various events."

She didn't stay long in Guam, however. "As you might imagine, it wasn't all that comfortable being one of very few women in that situation." At the conclusion of her service in Guam, she took a vacation trip to visit family friends in Japan. By that time, in 1955, American tourists were most welcome in Japan.

"Your Life is Defined by the People You Meet"– *Cathryn Hilker*

The University of Cincinnati is where Cathryn met the first of four people (other than her family) who had a profound influence on the direction of her life. The life experiences of these four influencers are linked to each other and to Cathryn by their respective journeys to discover, understand, and protect the shared global heritage of humans and animals.

Before celebrating these special connections, first a brief introduction to Cathryn's relationships with Dr. George Barbour, Dr. Byron Bernard, Dr. Louis Leakey, and Dr. Jane Goodall.

Dr. George Barbour was a geology professor and Dean of the College of Arts & Sciences at the University of Cincinnati (UC) while Cathryn was a student there. He was well known for the engaging gatherings hosted at his home, for inviting students to an evening of movies, and for serving food from around the world.

Sarah, Cathryn, and Jane Goodall (2002)

Her social time with Dr. Barbour and his wife is one of the things Cathryn remembers most vividly and fondly about her time at UC. She maintained her special connection with Dr. Barbour for many years after graduation, and to this day remains grateful for the contributions he made to the direction of her life.

A chance meeting of Dr. Byron Bernard during a 1956 lecture where he talked about an upcoming trip to Africa led to a rash decision that reshaped the rest of Cathryn's life. When Dr. Bernard invited Cathryn to join the trip, she said "yes" without a second thought and headed off with a man she barely knew. Dr. Bernard was at that time a part-time veterinarian at the Cincinnati Zoo.

During the same time period that Cathryn was gaining a life-altering experience in Africa, her favorite teacher, Dr. Barbour, was working with Dr. Louis Leakey, conducting field research to date discoveries of ancient remains of modern man in Southern Africa. When Dr. Leakey's African field work concluded in 1959, Dr. Barbour invited Leakey to make a stop in Cincinnati to deliver a talk during his United States tour.

Barbour invited Cathryn Hosea to join a dinner party at his home held in Leakey's honor. Dr. Leakey was quite impressed with Cathryn's poise, intelligence, and powers of observation. They hit it off immediately. He invited her to lead a study of chimpanzees in Africa for which he had recently secured funding. Cathryn remembers that Dr. Barbour strongly encouraged her to take the position, describing it as an "opportunity for greatness."

Cathryn said no. "My parents were horrified at the idea of me going alone to Africa for five years! I think if they had encouraged me even a little bit, I would have gone. I regretted that decision in that moment, but I do not regret the way my life has turned out. My beloved cheetahs have trusted me beyond reason. I wouldn't change that for anything."

Jane Goodall was tapped to lead Leakey's chimpanzee study. In July 1960, Goodall traveled from England to Tanzanyika (now Tanzania), venturing into the little-known world of wild chimpanzees. Goodall is one of the people Cathryn admires most in the world for her discoveries and for a lifetime of dedication to wildlife conservation. "I think Jane Goodall is one of the most influential people in the development of how we view ourselves. She is a remarkable human being, one of the most important people who has ever lived."

The stories of these four people—Dr. Barbour, Dr. Bernard, Dr. Leakey, and Dr. Goodall—and their collective impact on Cathryn Hilker's life, illuminate the essence of the person Cathryn has become, and reveal how her passions for Africa and wildlife conservation emerged and converged over a critical four-year period.

—∞ Discovering Africa with Dr. Byron Bernard [8] ∞—

In 1957, just shy of her 26th birthday, Cathryn Hosea made her first of what would be many trips to Africa. At the time, she was living at home with her parents and working at General Electric to earn money.

As Cathryn tells the beginning of this story, "I first met Dr. Byron Bernard, the Cincinnati Zoo's veterinarian, when he gave a talk to the Cincinnati Horse Show Association about his plans to deliver milk goats to Dr. Albert Schweitzer's medical mission in Africa. I could not believe my good luck to hear of an adventure I had only dared dream about: Africa."

She was hungry for another adventure after her experiences traveling to Guam and Japan, so after the talk she walked into the bar at the Vernon Manor Hotel in Avondale and sat down next to Dr. Bernard. He explained that he was preparing to depart from the Port of New Orleans to deliver Nubian milk goats donated by a local farmer. "I told him how badly I wanted to go to that nearly mystical continent. He quickly agreed to take me if I paid my share equally and didn't get in the way. I was thrilled!"

Cathryn was disappointed to learn that the trip plans would not include the opportunity to meet Dr. Schweitzer, but Dr. Bernard told her that other people were planning to join the African journey after the goats had been delivered. Cathryn's parents agreed to fund her airfare. She made plans to meet Dr. Bernard in Leopoldville, capital of the Belgian Congo, after he completed the goat-delivery mission.

In 1956-57, Dr. Bernard's missionary trip to deliver Nubian goats to Africa was big news in Cincinnati and beyond. The *Dairy Goat Journal*, a national bimonthly magazine now in its 98th year of publishing, chronicled the planning and fundraising for the mission. In its November/December 2017 issue, the magazine compiled an archival story from late 1956 through May 1957 called "The Gift of Goat Milk." The story is condensed and edited for brevity:[9]

> Dr. Albert Schweitzer, a German humanitarian and Nobel Peace Prize winner (1953), established a hospital in Lambaréné in what is now known as the African nation of Gabon.
>
> In the mid-1950s, Fred Knoop of Cincinnati, along with his wife Annette, formed the idea of sending dairy goats to Dr. Schweitzer to establish a herd to supply milk for the hospital. At the time, Fred Knoop was a vice-president of the American Milk Goat Record Association (AMGRA), now known as the American Dairy Goat

Dr. Schweitzer walks to his house with goats in Gabon, Lambaréné (1963); Photo courtesy of © AP/Shutterstock, Image #7333238a

Association. The effort became known as the 'Dairy Goats to Dr. Schweitzer' project.

In 1956 the Cincinnati Zoo assumed responsibility for the campaign to finance the trip, estimated to cost $8,000. Since only Nubian goats were wanted for this shipment, the Knoops encouraged breeders unable to supply stock to contribute cash toward the transportation of these animals. By March 1957, $2,000 had been raised by the Cincinnati Zoo and another $3,000 from the overseas relief program of the Evangelical and Reformed Church.

In May 1957 when the herd of 15 goats was assembled, the Studebaker-Packard Corporation donated a new truck which was then outfitted with stalls. The truck was used to transport the goats to New Orleans where it was loaded onto the steamship *Del Rio* to house the herd during passage. Transportation was donated by the Delta Steamship Lines, and the Ralston Purina Company donated a large quantity of Purina Goat Chow for use during the voyage.

By mid-June, the goats had been delivered to an appreciative Dr. Schweitzer, and Byron Bernard was ready to pursue part two of his Africa adventure. This part of the journey was documented in the *Cincinnati Enquirer*:

> When Dr. Bernard left Lambaréné, Dr. Schweitzer made him a present of Penelope, a West African sub-species, then just three years old. The gorilla had been a pet of Schweitzer's hospital personnel. Dr. Bernard provided her with a nice cozy cage for the 700-mile trip down the west coast of Africa to Leopoldville, but Penelope would have none of it. For three weeks she rode on the seat beside him as he drove and slept at night after pulling a sack over her head.[10]

What was not reported in various news articles or magazines was Dr. Bernard's plan to meet up with Cathryn Hosea at a hotel in Leopoldville.[11] In a history of the Cincinnati Zoo written by David Ehrlinger, he mentions that Dr. Bernard "was accompanied to Africa by a teenager, Cathryn Hosea."[12] But, in fact, when she met up with him in June after the goats were delivered to Dr. Schweitzer, she was just weeks shy of her 26th birthday on June 22nd.

As Cathryn remembers her somewhat unnerving arrival in Africa more than 60 years ago, "It was a long trip, flying alone to the Belgian Congo. I was a little worried. I didn't know whether Byron would actually show up, and I had no way to communicate with him. I had made up my mind, though: if he didn't show up, I would spend a few days in the Congo, see as much as I could, and then fly back home. That was my 'Plan B.'"

But Dr. Bernard did show up, climbing through the window of Cathryn's hotel room with Penelope still in tow. It was a defining moment to declare boundaries: Cathryn made it quite clear that she was there for a travel adventure, not for romance.

> I was six-foot-two at the time, and very capable of taking care of myself. But after that first calamitous night, Byron became my protector as we crossed the Congo and stayed in all kinds of crazy places. He generally introduced me as his younger sister. In retrospect, I think Dr. Bernard probably assumed I might accompany him as a 'girlfriend.' I was attractive and looked good for my age with long

blonde hair. I don't blame him for reading the situation that way, but he didn't know my father or my upbringing. I had no such intentions for that trip!

What did Cathryn's father think about her going on this trip? "I told him the truth about going to Africa, but Byron had said that there would be a group of people joining us on the trip. He even named them. They just didn't show up. I didn't tell my father about that part. I glossed over a lot of things."

On June 7, 1957, while still in Africa, Dr. Bernard let the Zoo know that he was sending the new gorilla home as a gift from Dr. Schweitzer, and that he was headed to the river port city of Brazzaville in French Equatorial Africa to ship her—unaccompanied—to Cincinnati.[13] Penelope was transported in a crate as cargo by air express.[14] In his remnant Alsatian/German accent, Dr. Schweitzer had called the gorilla "Penny-lope" which became her forever-name in Cincinnati.

According to Cincinnati Zoo Director Thane Maynard, "Penny-lope got to the Cincinnati Zoo in an era when zoos weren't breeding gorillas. They were even kept separate at zoos because of the potential that they would hurt each other. Penny-lope was the first animal to give birth at the Cincinnati Zoo. Her daughter Samantha, born in 1970, just recently died at age 50."

Cathryn and Dr. Bernard embarked on a 5,700-mile trek across the African continent to the east coast through the Belgian Congo, around Lake Victoria, and along the border between Tanganyika and Kenya to Mombasa. They spent a month making their way from Leopoldville to the Indian Ocean.

Cathryn filmed their adventure on a new 16 mm camera, a gift for the trip. Dr. Bernard promoted another bit of fiction, this time to the native people they met along the way. He explained the camera by saying that they were filming for the Walt Disney Company. Disney was known even in remote areas of Africa in the late 1950s.

This is Cathryn's oral history of her silent film describing their harrowing trip and the things they encountered along the way:

> We were constantly getting stuck in sand throughout the trip. We would have to get a shovel and hire some of the natives to dig us out.

You must picture this truck: it is the same one that Dr. Bernard used to deliver the goats to Dr. Schweitzer. It wasn't even a four-wheel drive!

The Congo is a rain forest, so there was a lot of water, around 140 inches a year. There were many tributaries of the Congo River that we had to cross to continue traveling east, and of course, no bridges. Again, we needed a lot of help from the native groups. They couldn't get across those rivers without help either because even the tributaries of the Congo River are very swift.

These wonderful people would congregate in groups along the shore of each river with a jury-rigged catamaran style boat—a flatbed tied with ropes on canoes—and they would just wait for people like us who needed help to get across the river. When there were enough people to make the trip worth the challenge of crossing the swift river, then we could depart.

We would drive the truck onto this makeshift boat, and then they would paddle us across to the other side while the river current was trying to sweep us away. The truck came close to falling in the river a few times. It could take as long as an hour to get across these rivers. And then a group of people on the other side of the river would have to pull us to shore with ropes at the landing spot, holding them while we drove the truck down temporary planks. We did this so many times! It wasn't a special service for us—it was just their way of transportation.

We did not eat any native food while we were traveling. We had our own food with us which consisted of mostly canned food—sardines and beer.

We were in awe of the arts and crafts we saw as we visited with various tribes. I especially loved the handmade instruments (music boxes) that children would play. They were made of tin on a board and created a wonderful sound. Sculptures of carved mahogany were magnificent, and very heavy. We bought two sculptures, of a man and a woman, which Dr. Bernard shipped back to the port of New Orleans on the goat truck. (Now my son Carl has the carved sculpture of the male figure in his home in San Francisco.)

We were also a bit unprepared for so many bare-breasted women, who would nurse their children as they went about their days, and even men who were completely nude. Everyone was barefoot. I gave several pairs of shoes to some native children, but they had to tear open the front to make room for their toes. We were also surprised, and concerned, about the swollen bellies of children, not from hunger, but from worms and other parasites. But that was the way of life then.

One special occasion was when we came upon a dramatic festival for the stately king and queen of the Watusi tribe (the former name of the Tutsi ethnic group in Rwanda, and the name of a popular dance craze in the 1960s). The Watusi tribe members are very tall, some over seven feet, and very thin! The king himself was nearly eight feet tall. Native horned cows engaged in what I would call a bull fight, followed by beautiful pageantry with dancing and drum performances. (The Watusis believed that cows were sacred and would only eat goats.)[16]

When they reached Mombasa, Dr. Bernard put their trusty goat truck on a ship back to New Orleans, caught a plane to the United States, and arrived back in Cincinnati on July 16 with a case of malaria. Cathryn was surprised by his sudden departure and decided to stay longer. "He just said to me 'sayonara, good luck.'[17] So what are you going to do? I got on a train to Nairobi and called this American guy I'd met along the way. He was a nice kid—he was very young—and he was very nice to host me at his home."

Although Cathryn's memories of that leg of the trip are a bit fuzzy 60 years later—without benefit of a home movie, photos, or a journal—she remembers fondly the experience of touring Nairobi and visiting national parks, especially Amboseli National Park at the base of Mt. Kilimanjaro in southern Kenya. It was there that she saw many wild animals including giraffes, zebras, cheetahs, and hundreds of bird species.

After only seeing cheetahs in captivity before that trip to Africa, Cathryn's first sighting of a cheetah in the wild in 1957 was a harbinger of things to come.

Dr. Louis Leakey, Jane Goodall, and "The Chimpanzee Project" [18]

The story of Cathryn Hosea's fateful exchange with Dr. Louis Leakey, arranged by Dr. George Barbour in 1959, is chronicled in a biography about Jane Goodall published in 2006 by Dale Peterson. This excerpt is provided with permission of the author.

🐾 Jane Goodall and Dr. Louis Leakey; Photo courtesy of © The Jane Goodall Institute, photo by Joan Travis

Back in Kenya in 1959, Louis Leakey had still been unable to locate an institutional sponsor for his proposed Chimpanzee Project, so he finally turned away from the typical sources of funding to ask for a grant from his atypical American friend, Leighton Wilkie.

Wilkie began funding some of Leakey's work starting with a check for $1,000 in 1955 to help with the digging at Olduvai.[19] The support continued each year during 1957 through 1959.

In February 1959, Leakey requested another grant to underwrite a Chimpanzee Project in Tanganyika, slated to begin in September. In a quick, enthusiastic response, Wilkie noted that the foundation was prepared to underwrite the "very interesting" Chimpanzee Project.

On July 17, 1959, Louis and Mary Leakey were starting their yearly excavations at Olduvai, and they had for the first time decided to start digging in the lowest strata of the gorge. Louis was in bed with the flu, but Mary went off with their two Dalmatians to sniff around some nearby exposures. "It seemed to be part of a skull," Mary wrote in her autobiography, *Disclosing the Past*. "They *were* hominid."

Ultimately, they recovered four hundred fragments, which Mary painstakingly glued together into three major inter-locking pieces that together presented a haunting visage, at once apelike and humanoid, with an upper palate notable for its large grinding molars. Finally, after an extended comparison of his skull with samples from the two known *australopithecine genera*, Louis concluded that he and Mary had found the remains of an individual from a third genus and, as he was soon to announce, "the oldest yet discovered maker of stone tools."

Louis and Mary became instant celebrities. Louis was invited to speak at a conference at the University of Chicago in November 1959 designed to celebrate the centennial of Darwin's *Origin of Species*. On his way to the United States, Louis stopped off in London to make a presentation to the Academy of Sciences. Jane Goodall attended the lecture, and later dined with Louis Leakey at which point he revealed "that the grant from Leighton Wilkie had finally come through." On November 7, Jane wrote to her friend Bernard Verdcourt, a botanist who directed the herbarium of the Coryndon Museum in Nairobi, that "the Chimp project is fixed for next June."

But in spite of his reassurances to Jane, Leakey may have been contemplating a serious betrayal. While he was in the states, he had attended a dinner in Cincinnati given by George Barbour, a geology professor and dean of students at the University of Cincinnati. Barbour was a kind, sympathetic man who had invited a young woman named Cathryn Hosea to the event. He telephoned her, as Hosea remembers, to say, "A friend of mine, Louis Leakey, is joining us for dinner" and to express the opinion that Dr. Leakey might be able to connect her with a job opportunity.

Hosea immediately liked Louis. He seemed "so kind, such a gentleman." Following the meal, he lectured at the University of Cincinnati, and she was overwhelmed, struck not only by his greatness but by his patience and apparent humility, his "incredible willingness to stay and be asked questions. If a child wanted to ask a question, he would get down on the floor to give an answer."

Louis knew by then that Cathryn Hosea wanted to get to Africa and was looking for some kind of anthropology job, and at the end of the Cincinnati lecture he told her he was going to the University of Chicago next and arranged to meet her there. She attended the Chicago lecture, and then they met in his hotel room. They sat on the bed, talking about Africa. Louis had long before developed his skills in simple performance tricks, minor acts of prestidigitation and string finger manipulations, which had served him well when meeting new people in Africa and elsewhere. Now, talking to the young woman, he pulled out some string and began demonstrating a few string-figure stories. At the same time, he told her about a group of chimpanzees living in a very remote place beside a lake, and then about his desire to send someone there to study the apes in their natural environment. Years ago, he had sent a man out there, Louis declared, but the poor fellow simply did not have the staying power and patience. Now Louis had decided to send a woman because women had more patience. It would be an exciting, demanding job in a very remote, very inaccessible place, and therefore she would have to have her appendix out.[19] Was she prepared to do that?

While continuing to demonstrate the shape-shifting string figures, Louis also mentioned his young secretary at the Coryndon Museum, Jane Goodall. As Hosea recalls the words, he said "There is a young girl in my office who wants the job in the worst way. But she doesn't have the credentials."

Louis went on. Miss Hosea would need someone, another non-African, to accompany her. That was, unfortunately, one of the requirements of the stuffy colonial administrator, though ultimately not so significant. More importantly, she would always have an African support staff, and therefore in spite of the remoteness of the place, she would be safe and well cared for as she studied the wild chimpanzees. It was going to be a unique, extremely challenging job.

At some point in this discussion, Louis stopped talking and fiddling with the string figures, handed her the string, and said, "I want you to do what I just did." It was a typical L.S.B. Leakey test of observational abilities, and she repeated the sequence of figures he had just produced. He said, "You'll do just fine. How would you like to come to Africa to do a chimpanzee study?"

Louis thus offered her the very job he had long been promising to Jane. He seemed to be entirely serious about the offer, and during the months that followed he maintained a steady correspondence on the subject with Cathryn Hosea while keeping it a secret from Jane in London. His explanation to Hosea was straightforward and reasonable: she had credentials—an undergraduate degree in anthropology.

Louis, of course, had an iconoclast's intuitive disdain for the abstract navigations represented by the academic degree, and he understood only too well that the qualities fundamental to success in a long-term field study were passion and character. The job would require above all an unteachable endurance and a high tolerance for isolation, tedium, and danger. Jane had already shown that she was a suitable candidate on that level. She could do the job. But, after all, what would that job mean if no one was interested in the results? Whoever went out to conduct this project would be representing him, and she would need not merely to find the apes, to watch them, to learn something about them. She would also have to succeed in convincing others, scientists above all, of the value of what she had done. How could that young, pretty, enthusiastic, animal-loving former secretary of his, now living in London, possibly translate any observations from the forests of Tanganyika into a result that would be respected by the scientific community at large?

While Louis had gone silent in his correspondence with Jane, in fact, he was still exchanging letters with Cathryn Hosea, who was agonizing over that amazing job offer of studying wild chimpanzees in Tanganyika. The young American longed to go to Africa (again), but the lack of a concrete vision of what the project might entail, combined with Louis's unreasonable insistence that she commit herself for five years, finally led her to decline what she nevertheless recognized was "the opportunity of a lifetime."

On May 31, 1960, Jane Goodall postponed her recently announced wedding and headed to Africa to study chimpanzees. The rest is history.

—❦❦❦ *The Fabulous Four* ❦❦❦—

Dr. George Barbour *1890–1977* [20]

Born in Edinburgh, Scotland, George Barbour was internationally renowned on four continents for his work as a geologist.

After attending University of Cambridge, where he earned both B.A. and M.A degrees, Barbour headed to the United States in 1919 to attend Columbia University. He had met Dorothy Dickinson during an earlier visit to New York, married her upon graduation in 1920, and immediately accepted a position to establish the geology department at Yenching University in Peking (now Beijing). A religious couple, both George and Dorothy were commissioned by the London Missionary Society for humanitarian service in China.

During his time in Peking, Barbour conducted geological research and field studies. Through this avenue he met and worked with W. C. Pei, V. K. Ting, and Wong Wen-Hao, who were conducting the "Geological Survey of China," best known for the team's discovery of the hominid and associated bones of *Synanthropus*, or Peking Man, from an era 650,000 years ago.

Barbour was a pioneer in long-distance learning, completing his PhD from Columbia University in 1929. Shortly after, however, his growing family was forced to move back to the United States when the eldest of three sons contracted "Peking fever." Unable to return to Peking due to the political revolution in China, Barbour accepted a short-term position at the University of Cincinnati where he taught geology and in 1938 was named Dean of the College of Arts & Sciences (a position he held for 20 years).

A second area of field work for Dr. Barbour was in South Africa, helping to date important finds with the researchers who discovered the Men-Apes of Africa. He worked with Raymond A. Dart, of the University of the Witwatersrand, South Africa, who discovered the first *Australopithecus* (Southern Ape) dating back 2-to-4 million years ago from which the genus *homo*, or modern man, is thought to be descended. And he also made three trips to Africa from 1954 to 1959 with researchers E. J. Wayland and Dr. Louis Leakey.

Although Dr. Barbour was living in Louisville at the time of his death, his memorial was held at the University of Cincinnati. According to his eldest son Hugh, "He was remembered by former students and colleagues as scholar and composer, as 'my Dean,' as the pipe-smoking professor, and for his humor, wise administration, and inspiring teaching."[21]

Dr. George Barbour

Dr. Byron W. Bernard *1917–2006*

Known to many as "Doc," Dr. Byron Bernard was the part-time veterinarian at the Cincinnati Zoo & Botanical Garden, as well as an animal hospital owner in Cincinnati and Northern Kentucky, for many years. A favorite story about Dr. Bernard (in addition to the 1957 trip with Cathryn to Africa and Dr. Schweitzer's gift of a gorilla named Penelope) was memorialized in a 1960 *Enquirer* article[22]: "It's understandable that people often think they've had one too many when they stop at a traffic light, casually glance at the convertible next to them, and see—double-take—a GORILLA wearing a large sun hat!" At the time, Penelope was seven years old and weighed 130 pounds.

Penelope and Dr. Byron Bernard

Clearly, Dr. Bernard had a great sense of humor in addition to a passion for adventure. Penelope was a frequent visitor to Dr. Bernard's home where his African treasures from 1957 were on display, including a pair of wood sculptures—one for Cathryn, and one for Dr. Bernard.

Dr. Louis Leakey *1903–1972*

Dr. Louis Leakey, together with his wife Mary, is best remembered for the couple's great contributions to the world's knowledge about our earliest ancestors.

Louis Leakey was born in Kabete, Kenya, and raised by missionary parents during his early years among the Kikuyu people. He attended St. John's College of Cambridge University, studying anthropology and archaeology, earning his doctorate in African prehistory. When he returned home to Africa, his interests shifted to paleoanthropology (the branch of anthropology that deals with fossil hominids). That shift in focus led him to Olduvai Gorge in what is now Tanzania. The geology of the area was already well known and originally thought to be from the Pleistocene era about 600,000 years ago. It was there that the team discovered hominid fossils that were millions of years old, linking them to human evolution, including *H. habilis* and *H. erectus*.

🐾 Louis and Mary Leakey in Olduvai

Mary Nicol, an archaeologist who married Dr. Leakey in 1937, is also known for her work in researching fossil remains. In 1948, on Rusinga Island, Mary Leakey discovered *Proconsul africanus*, an ancestor of both apes and humans that existed 18-25 million years ago. She also worked the Olduvai site in 1959, famously discovering a human fossil named *Zinjanthropus-bosei*, estimated to be nearly two million years old, on a day when Louis was home sick with the flu. This quest for fossils was a family enterprise. The Leakeys' son Jonathan made yet another major discovery in 1960: *homo habilis*, at that time humanity's earliest discovered ancestor.

After WWII, Dr. Leakey became curator of the Coryndon Memorial Museum in Nairobi. It was through his connections at this museum that he met Jane Goodall, a young assistant who worked there and who he hired to carry out The Chimpanzee Project.

Dr. Leakey devoted his later years to mentoring Ms. Goodall as well as Dian Fossey, who studied gorillas, and to writing and lecturing. Having suffered from headaches and epilepsy for some years, he died at age 69.

Dr. Jane Goodall, DBE *b. 1934–* [23]

When Jane Goodall first entered the forest of Gombe, the world knew very little about chimpanzees, and even less about their unique genetic kinship to humans. She took an unorthodox approach in her field research, immersing herself in their habitat and their lives to experience their complex society as a neighbor rather than a distant observer. She came to understand them not only as a species, but also as individuals with emotions and long-term bonds. Dr. Goodall's discovery in 1960 that chimpanzees make and use tools is considered one of the greatest achievements of twentieth-century scholarship. She redefined traditional conservation with an approach that recognized the central role people play in the well-being of animals and habitat.

In 1965, Goodall completed a Ph.D. in ethology from the University of Cambridge, one of very few people to do so without having first completed an undergraduate degree. In 1977, she founded the Jane Goodall Institute to support the research in Gombe and scale up the protection of chimpanzees

Dr. Jane Goodall, DBE; Photo Courtesy of © The Jane Goodall Institute, photo by Bill Wallauer

in their habitats. The rapidly growing problem of deforestation and declining chimpanzee populations across Africa required a new solution.

In 1991, when a group of young people confided their own deep conservation concerns, she invited them to create Roots & Shoots, a program engaging young people in 100 countries to foster an informed generation of conservation leaders.

Today, Dr. Jane Goodall encourages each of us to "use the gift of our life to make the world a better place." As a conservationist, humanitarian, and crusader for the ethical treatment of animals, she is a global force for compassion and was named a UN Messenger of Peace the same year she was awarded the title of Dame of the British Empire.

In 2009, Dr. Goodall published a book called *Hope for Animals and Their World* offering global case examples of the ways in which many endangered species are being successfully rescued. Cincinnati Zoo Director and co-author Thane Maynard shared field notes from Mongolia, Indonesia, Colombia, and Trinidad. Maynard also wrote a forward to the book[24] which he called "Jane's Feather," excerpted with permission here:

> The idea for a book of hopeful stories about wildlife was launched on an autumn evening in 2002. In the middle of a public lecture at a sold-out basketball arena of six thousand people, Jane stepped away from the podium and said her classic line, 'Let me tell you a story . . . '
>
> Reaching behind the podium, Jane slowly pulled out the largest feather I'd ever seen; indeed, one of the largest feathers in the world. It was a primary feather from a California condor, the most endangered animal in America. She told the enthralled gathering that she carried it with her for inspiration because it reminded her that many species are coming back from the brink of extinction thanks to the hard work of a great spectrum of experts, activists, students, and enthusiasts.
>
> Diversity is what holds our world steady.
>
> This book is a starting point to share the hope of such a dream in which people of all ages, from all over the world and from all walks of life, show that it is possible to help, rather than harm, the rest of the

world around us. For it is not counter to human nature to be hopeful. In fact, it is quite the opposite—it is essential to our nature.

This sort of passion is represented in nearly every effective conservationist I have ever known. It is the truly passionate conservationists who *never* give up. We need guiding lights—role models—who can light the way. The scope of influence from Jane's cover stories in 1960s *National Geographic*, early TV specials about her life among the wild chimpanzees, and her seminal research chronicled in her 1971 book *In the Shadow of Man*, encompassed much more than just reporting Jane's scientific accomplishments. Her long-term study of wildlife . . . also changed the way men and women viewed the possibilities of their own lives and careers.

The generations of researchers and conservationists in this book share this in common: they refuse to give up or take no for an answer.

Carl "Hege" and Cathryn Hilker (2005)

3

Where the Wild Things Are

∞

When despair for the world grows in me
and I wake in the night at the least sound
in fear of what my life and my children's lives may be,
I go and lie down where the wood drake
rests in his beauty on the water, and the great heron feeds.
I come into the peace of wild things
who do not tax their lives with forethought
of grief. I come into the presence of still water.
And I feel above me the day-blind stars
waiting with their light. For a time
I rest in the grace of the world, and am free.
—*Excerpt from "The Peace of the Wild Things" by Wendell Barry*

Back in Cincinnati and living on her parents' Mason farm after her momentous trip to Africa, Cathryn seized an unusual opportunity to raise her first large cat. She was between jobs at the time, sorting out next steps while enjoying the time to ride her horses.

The Cincinnati Zoo's former director, Bill Hoff,[25] needed to figure out a temporary home for one of the Zoo's young tigers and offered the caretaker "job" to Cathryn. It was the first wild animal in captivity (of many) she helped to raise.[26] The experience of hosting Toughy the Tiger on the farm was just the tip of the iceberg for Cathryn, launching her into a lifetime of husbandry, learning, and teaching.[27]

A year later, in 1963, Cathryn began teaching English in the Mason, Ohio, public school system. After two years, she shifted teaching jobs to

Cathryn and Toughy the Tiger in Mason, Ohio

her alma mater, known then as Hillsdale High School and today as The Seven Hills School.[28] In retrospect, it is easy to see how these years spent teaching in a classroom both verified how far Cathryn had come in her own capabilities, and also created a pathway for a not-yet-imagined future as the Zoo's star cat ambassador.

Along the way, Cathryn had developed a passion for poetry and Shakespeare that she could indulge fully as a teacher at Hillsdale. During the 1965–66 school year, she taught English and literature. Cathryn's memory of that experience is that "I had a wonderful time. Those kids were so brilliant, and they were marvelous to deal with. We read *Hamlet* when they were only in the 10th grade, and they really understood it. But I was uncomfortable teaching as a colleague with the people who had been my own teachers, so I only taught there for one year."

Answering the Call of the Wild
The Remarkable Life of Cathryn Hosea Hilker

The Wild Thing Himself:
Carl Frederick "Hege" Hilker, Jr. 1935–2016

It's been an interesting life! —Cathryn Hilker

"To say Carl was eccentric was an understatement. He lived life on his own terms, marched to his own beat, and found joy in pursuits of life that others give up for more 'traditional' paths of contentment. Yet, it was the eccentric way that he found his joy that ultimately is remembered most and appreciated."[29]

Son Carl says that his dad "liked being unique. He loved being eccentric, and anyone who knew him could related to that. He sort of fed off of it." Carl elaborates by saying that his father was quite intelligent, but that he wasn't very driven. "He was good at a lot of things, but never became expert at anything—except flying perhaps." Hege ran the New York Marathon eight times, once on crutches due to degenerative arthritis, and raced in ski marathons around the world.

🐾 Hege Hilker

Hege's family background provides some insight into the roots of his eccentricity. Carl's nickname "Hege" was borrowed from his mother's family name, even though Hegeland was not part of his given name.

To set the stage, Ella Hegeland was born in Arizona in 1903. She was married three times. At age 24, in 1927, she married Jacob Moerlein of Cincinnati beer-family fame. Jacob Moerlein died in a crash in September 1931, leaving Ella a widow to care for an infant (George Moerlein). About a year later, in October 1932, Ella married Carl F. Hilker, and Carl Jr. (who we now know as "Hege") was born about three years later, in July 1935.

Ella Hegeland Moerlein Hilker and Carl Hilker, Sr. divorced at some point prior to 1951 which is the year Ella married third husband Gilbert Roth Symons. Hege's mother died in 1983 at age 80, and Gil Symons passed away in 2005 at age 94.

Cathryn's speculation on Hege's eccentric ways falls into two buckets of possibility. The first is that his family didn't pay much attention to him. "His last name wasn't Moerlein. His mother had inherited a lot of money when her husband was killed, but his half-brother George got the attention." Compounding this situation was that the Hilker marriage apparently wasn't a good one.

Ella had inherited the Moerlein family property in Glendale—a farm at that time—which was, according to Carl III, "a country party house." During and after his grandmother's marriage to Carl Hilker, Ella continued to live on the Moerlein property.

Carl III says "from my earliest memory, my paternal grandparents (Carl, Sr. and Ella Hilker) were divorced. He re-married into a bit of money, so he really didn't have to work that much." Carl, Sr. married Mary Hinsch Baumgardner in 1947. She was the daughter of Charles A. Hinsch, Sr., founder of Fifth Third Bank (as we know it today). "My grandfather played golf and spent time in Florida." In 1973, Carl, Sr., was married a third time, to Caroline Rinehart.

Hege's privileged upbringing led him to attend college and study geology at Dartmouth. "He was really a brilliant man," according to Cathryn. "He went to Dartmouth because the college encourages people to be a little odd, I think."

In the 1950s, Hege joined the Navy for about two years. He focused on aviation, but in a post-war era, the Navy downsized and discharged a great number of airmen. But he continued to fly as a civilian and develop his interest in flying...and in Cathryn! Carl III states:

> My mom was extremely attractive as a young adult. When you see pictures of her, she probably could have been a model. She was very tall, very straight, very slender, very elegant looking.
>
> I think it was a case of opposites attract. My mom was probably attracted to him because he was a handsome-looking guy. He was a little bit wild and playful, and she probably thought that was kind of fun. But my mom's father never liked my dad. His perspective was that you should work hard, and if you don't work, you're a bum.
>
> My Dad used to love buzzing people at parties. If he knew someone was having a party, he would get a huge kick out of diving the plane at their house repeatedly until they came outside waving furiously.

Cathryn's characterization of her father's feelings toward Hege is even stronger. She said "My father never called him by name. His name was Carl, but my dad always called him 'that son of a bitch.' Hege used to fly over our house and cut the engine so you didn't hear him coming. Then he would fly right over the garden where my father was sitting, and Dad would go 'goddammit.'"

"The love of Carl's life was flying. Anything that afforded lift into the sky he either flew or wished he had—from planes and helicopters to hot air balloons. He was also an avid sky diver who once jumped out of the back of a decommissioned 727 to commemorate a famous bank robber who had used such an exploit to escape capture. Had he lived in the pioneering era of the barnstormers in biplanes, there is little doubt he would have been the first up in the morning and the last to leave the sky."[30]

Cathryn's memories of Hege's passion for flying are vividly scary. "He was a wonderful pilot. But my husband was a madman. He used to scare me to death. I used to say, 'if you do that again I will throw up.' So that's exactly what he did! He would put the plane into a steep dive, and because of the G-force, I was pressured back. And then I did throw up. He once flew a plane upside down under a bridge on the Ohio River. He would fly over Victoria Falls in Zambia. He had a short landing strip in a field on our farm. He flew the night mail, which was very dangerous, but he liked doing it because it was

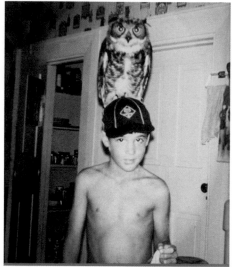

Carl, Cathryn, and Hege with Hooty the Horned Owl

quiet. He could probably have been in jail a million times. It was insane."

In Dayton, Hege was known for piloting hot air balloons at the Dayton International Air Shows and firing a cannon to start half marathons. According to the *Dayton Daily News*, "All the car alarms in downtown Dayton went off."[31]

Although Hege did not fully share Cathryn's passion for animals, he tried to up his game for her. "He was not an animal person or lover. It's not that he disliked animals. I think he appreciated them because it helped that eccentric lifestyle. I introduced him to fox hunting. He couldn't ride worth a nickel, but at least he kept the horse under him. Hege would be leaning over in the wrong position and I'd have to yell at him to straighten up."

One of the Hilker family's animal stories was so amazing that it was reported in *The Western Star* (a now-defunct newspaper).[32] As it was reported in 1978, "Have you had a horned owl perch on your telephone lately? Carl and Cathryn Hilker of Mason have. The owl, technically a wild creature, flies from the telephone to the top of the refrigerator and then to Carl's shoulder in the kitchen of their home. It lands ever so gracefully on the man's shoulder."

In her Own Words: Meeting and Marrying the Wild Thing

I met Hege Hilker at a formal dinner party at a good friend's house to celebrate her daughter's engagement. I thought they said his name was Peggy. I only mention that it was formal—long white tablecloth, china, sterling, long-stemmed glasses—because what happened as we sat down even now seems inappropriate to its circumstances.

This man at the other side of the table clinked his glass to get our attention stood up and repeated what had to be one of the dirtiest jokes I have ever heard. This was greeted by total silence. Then my friend said, 'Thank you, Hege, for your remarks. Now let's all enjoy the dinner prepared for us.'

I went home that night thinking, 'I've never met anybody named Peggy.' He had just returned from out West doing some insane thing, and he had a broken leg—a spiral break from skiing—and couldn't walk on it for a year. He

Engagement Portrait December 1968

had a cast on his leg, and he was so proud of it that he annoyed me. I mean, everybody was signing his cast and I thought, 'You are not right in the head,' because he really wasn't. You would think I had learned my lesson at that moment, but he was quite good looking. He looked like a pirate. He looked like Clark Gable, like a movie star.

The first time I ever had a date with him, he called me at like midnight to ask me if I wanted to go flying. I am embarrassed to say that I was still living at home in my mid-thirties. I said, 'Yes, when?' and Hege said, 'Now.' We flew all over with the engine off and it scared me to death. He just did insane things, but he was a competent flier.

Every time Hege left, I never knew if I'd see him again. One time I didn't hear from him for weeks. This was after we were engaged for heaven sakes. I called the airport in Hamilton and asked the owner, Bill Hogan, if he'd seen Hege lately. I still remember Bill saying, 'Cathryn, didn't he call you?' And I said, 'No, the last I heard he was coming home for dinner, but I haven't seen him in days.' Well, Hege had gone to Spain to deliver a plane and wouldn't be back for a couple of weeks because the plane was a wreck and needed a lot of work. I mean he just didn't have a lot of good sense.

I knew him for two years before we married on May 17, 1969. I never could remember the exact date.

"Later in life, fueled by his wife Cathryn's career in wildlife conservation, Carl became an avid supporter—in both time and money. In the '90s these efforts focused on cheetahs and the African country of Namibia. With Carl's conceptual and financial support, the two of them were able to buy an initial large parcel of land (and later a second parcel) which created a bulkhead for conservation efforts to save these big cats in the wild. It was this purchase that helped establish what is now the largest conservancy effort to protect and study Cheetahs in the wild, the Cheetah Conservation Fund (CCF)."[33]

Cathryn's version of Hege's relationship with CCF[34] adds lively color to this story: "My husband was a wild man, and he was insane to live with. But he was very generous. When CCF's founder and director Dr. Laurie Marker wanted to buy this place in Namibia in 1995, nobody could come up with a million dollars in one week. That farm was going to be bought by people who wanted to turn it into a hunting lodge because there are leopards on the high Waterberg Plateau where this farm ends. Laurie wanted this specific place to stop the hunting immediately to save the leopards. But somebody had to come up with a million dollars in seven days, so Hege just said 'I'll buy it.' He did that, and he built an airstrip for them, but that was really for himself. He used to fly upside down to approach the landing strip in Namibia. It looked like he was going to crash into the Waterberg Plateau. Laurie named it Hilkerdom."

Dr. Marker couldn't agree more. "Hege had a heart of gold. It felt like we were in the fight to save cheetahs together, like family." In hearing this story as he was growing up, son Carl III came to understand that his father had a big vision for the Namibian initiative, and was a risk-taker, so buying the property at the eleventh hour came as no surprise to Carl.

∞ Son Carl Hilker III (b. 1970) ∞

Cathryn was an older mom, certainly by 1970 standards. She was 39 when Carl III was born in July. He was mostly raised on the same farm where his mother grew up and where his Hosea grandparents still lived, although he was more social and not really a farm kid like his mother. "My mom

🐾 Carl, Cathryn, Danica, and Alice Hilker (2019)

introduced me to horses, but I never really cared for them that much. Horses were her passion. She was always more comfortable with animals than with people. Before she had me, she did a lot of show jumping. But after I was born, she switched to dressage which is comparatively speaking a safer sport."

Carl attended college in the San Francisco Bay area, specializing in community mental health working with children and adolescents. He is a Licensed Clinical Psychologist and has worked for Kaiser Permanente since 2006. Carl says that "growing up in a large extended family in a rural environment helped develop my life-long interest in family dynamics and behavior." He lives with his wife, Alice, and two daughters, Cathryn and Danica, in the San Francisco Bay area.

—∞ *Stories From the Vault* ∞—

Cathryn's Favorite Stories

"My son didn't really like my cats, and they returned the favor: they didn't like him. But because he was a little kid, and I couldn't leave him alone at the farm, I made him come to the Zoo with me on weekends when he was not in

🐾 Left: Christmas with Angel (mid-1980s); Right: (clockwise from top left) Grandpa Hosea, Gil Symons, Hege, and young Carl (mid-1980s)

school. I would lock him in the ferret cage to keep him safe while I was busy doing other things. Sometimes his friend Augie would come along.

"A visitor would go to the education director and say, 'Sir, do you know that there is a young child in the ferret cage in the Discovery Center?' And their response would be, 'Oh, that's okay. We know that. He's Cathryn's helper.' Can you imagine what they would do now? Some do-gooder would have me sued for mistreatment of a child or have me jailed. I actually made a list of the other things I did that wouldn't fly today, like raising two lions, a cheetah, a mountain lion/cougar, a great horned owl, and a tiger in our house.

"I used to drive back and forth to the Zoo in my beast of a car—a Chevette—that was held together with chewing gum. If you cranked the window down too hard, the whole thing would come off in your hands and the window wouldn't come up again. The year that Angel lived with me, the only place she would sit in that car was right behind me. I didn't use a cage. She used to like to comb my hair with her teeth. It didn't bother me if she pulled out a few hairs, but I had much longer hair then so I could cover up the bare ring

Answering the Call of the Wild
The Remarkable Life of Cathryn Hosea Hilker

it left on my scalp, and it gave her something to do on the drive. So that was Angel's place. If you sat there, God help you. Carrie Cougar always called for the front seat. If you tried to move her, she would just go limp so you couldn't move her. Only a mountain lion can do that.

"We were going home one day after Carl had been locked in the ferret cage and I'd finished all my talks. On my way home I saw a motorcycle-policeman behind me and thought, 'Oh my God, what have I done?' I wasn't going over the speed limit because I drive about 15 miles an hour. So he pulls up in front of me and motions me to pull over to the side. He came up to the window, tipped his hat, and leaned in the window. Before I could say a word, my mountain lion jumped from her seat, tore the handle off the window—and of course the window falls down—so she ends up with her whole front end hanging out of the car to say hello to this new person.

"I used to drop off and pick up Carl at Summit Country Day with Angel in the back seat and the mountain lion in the front seat. Carl also wedged into the front seat with the cat. Everybody used to come to the door to see Carl arrive because the cat would fall out the door onto the pavement while Carl got out of the car, and then climb back in. The cat was tied to the door so she couldn't get loose. Well, then it got to be so popular that everybody would come over to see Carl's mother and the cat. They thought it was pretty neat that Carl was living with all those animals. Carl didn't really see it that way. He finally said, 'Mother, please don't come to school anymore. Can't I meet you around the block?'"

Carl III's Favorite Stories

"One of the stresses growing up as Cathryn's son was that she was never really thinking about buying me cool clothes. I was a kid and I want to be cool like the rest of the kids. So back in the early eighties I wanted a Polo or Izod shirt with the collar swept up. But my mom would always say, 'Why do you want that stuff?' It just wasn't part of her world. She didn't get it. Kris Kalnow, who was working with my mom at that time, had to step in. She told Mom that she had to take me shopping to get some real clothes so I could fit in like the other kids. Mom still thought that fitting in was my choice and had nothing to do with my choice of clothes.

"My friend Augie and I rode in the back of that Chevette, with a cheetah in the back trying to eat our ice cream while we screamed and yelled at my mother to do something about the cat. If we stopped at a drive through to get ice cream or some food, the cheetah would poke its head out of the window to stare at the person handing us our purchases. I was embarrassed to go to school in Mom's car because it was full of duct tape. The seats, the headrests, everything had to be duct-taped. There was cat hair everywhere. It was ridiculous! And it was definitely comedic. Her job required a lot of mundane tasks like cleaning cat cages, but one of the unique pleasures—a sort of oddity—was being able to drive around with your cheetah in your car. It was strange, but there were no laws against it at the time. You couldn't have a pet raccoon at home, but you could have a pet mountain lion or cheetah. That cat really wanted nothing to do with me.

"After taking animals to schools for several years, Mom asked (Zoo Director) Ed Maruska if she could have a lion to raise at home on the farm. He said no for a long time, but he finally said yes. (Mom says she thinks that Maruska agreed to this arrangement because she was driving him nuts and to teach her a lesson about the challenges of raising a big wild animal.) So we had two lions from birth through about nine months. They lived in our house, basically growing up with me, and my mom drove them back and forth in her car to the Zoo every day. In some ways, my childhood memories are more affected by lions than cheetahs because they are a little more playful. You can wrestle with them. After about nine months a lion becomes too aggressive and potentially very dangerous, so they went back to the Zoo to live out their lives."

The Hilkers' Dream House

In September 1999, the Hilkers' "dream house" was featured in *Cincinnati Magazine*. The condensed story by Jane Durell called "Where The Wild Things Are," together with photographs by David Steinbrunner, is shared with permission of *Cincinnati Magazine.* [35]

Carl and Cathryn Hilker live in a house that sits as lightly within the trees of the 50 acres as some wild creature come to rest. Windows are generous and uncurtained, the roofline leaps and plunges, handsome hardwood floors are covered here and there with African rugs.

Like many expansive ideas, this one began simply. Their first plan was to add one large room to their small house in rural Warren County to accommodate a cheetah carrousel given to them by a friend. But as they planned, their vision expanded. In the end, the Hilkers have a new home in the woods, a quarter mile across the fields from the original house.

Cathryn's early guidelines to architect Christopher Knoop and his associate Bert Ring were clear, but not specific. "I'd like to feel as though I'm sitting in the woods under an umbrella," she told them. "Hanging furniture would suit me because I don't want to fuss. I'd like to be able to clean with a hose."

The Hilkers call their new home Narnia, after the mythical land in C. S. Lewis's *The Lion, the Witch, and the Wardrobe*. "A friend suggested it, and now we have the name on the entrance post," Cathryn says. "But," she adds, "we need a lion sculpture somewhere."

She's referring, of course, to Aslan, the Lion King of Narnia, whom Lewis described as "wild, you know." The lion sculpture is perfectly at home here, where tree stumps carved as The Three Bears greet visitors, a small bronze cougar in mid-pounce peeks through the trees, and the forked trunk of a dead tree remains, transformed as a winged eagle rising with a snake.

Cathryn is known for her role as director of the Cincinnati Zoo's Cat Ambassador Program. Carl, a pilot "licensed to fly anything but blimps," owns a small aviation support company.

"If ever clients deserved an individual house, the Hilkers do. They are quite remarkable people," says their architect. Looking over the Hilkers' property, Knoop saw that beyond the field, then designated as the building site, lay a woods that could be cleared of undergrowth, good trees saved, and a house fitted in. The Hilkers would have the views they wanted and a better setting. A swamp lay between the field and the new location; now it has become a pond with an unusual architect-designed, cantilevered dock.

The owners' unique preoccupations are announced at the front door, where a long vertical stretch of glass is bordered by Honduras mahogany carved in low relief. A cheetah leaps across the bottom panel; behind it is a suggestion of Carl's farm in Namibia, Africa, which is headquarters for the Cheetah Conservation Fund Center, a project deeply important to the couple. A second cheetah, partially hidden, and a cougar appear on the door's side panels, as well as a DC-3, a biplane, an antique and a modern parachute and Cathryn, barely visible, on the back of a long-beloved horse. Madeira woodcarver P.K. Smith designed and executed the project. "They

Answering the Call of the Wild
The Remarkable Life of Cathryn Hosea Hilker

gave me photographs to work from, and I combined those elements into a collage. It was a real task."

Sky is readily visible through windows that frame views in all directions. Interior walls on the ground floor are minimal, so almost all directions are at hand. A soaring central room rises to 30 feet at one side, above a balcony lined with bookshelves.

Colors, taking their cue from the couple's many handloomed Namibian rugs, are the muted shades of Africa, and much of the art reflects that continent. Paintings show an elephant moving through the grass, people in a thatched-hut village, cheetahs contemplating the world. A

Art Imitates Life: Live Cheetah Moya and Fireplace Echo

couple giraffe figures stand about, less than life-size, but eye-to-eye with a human.

The Hilkers are endlessly hospitable, (but) not all of their guests are people. Kat, a black-and white house cat, winters with the Hilkers but in summer lives at the Zoo and takes part in Cathryn's cat shows there. Now and then a cheetah is brought out to run. "When a mountain lion grows up, you can't turn them loose, but cheetahs are sight-hunters and nothing distracts them from a lure," explained Cathryn. The lure she uses is a teddy bear, tied to a car wheel and bounced across a field at approximately cheetah-speed. To accommodate such a houseguest, the home has a basement that can be made cheetah-proof in seconds.

Angel and Carrie Cougar at the Cheetah Encounter, Cincinnati Zoo; sculpture by Tom Tsuchiya (2010)

4

Innovation and Determination

—⊗—

The girl does not take no for an answer.
—Thane Maynard, Zoo Director

Cathryn Hosea Hilker is one of a kind. She is the only person to have worked as a volunteer and/or paid staff member with four consecutive Cincinnati Zoo directors.[36]

Nearly 60 years ago she put her toe in the water as a wild cat trainer with Director Bill Hoff and Toughy the Tiger. On her own, she created a one woman speaker's bureau, showing the 16mm film she took during her 1957 trip to Africa with Dr. Bernard to community groups who had only dreamed of such an adventure. In the early 1970s, she started volunteering to promote the Zoo to potential members, and was later employed as a trainer, educator, and ambassador for cats during the years Ed Maruska and Gregg Hudson served as directors. Although she continued to go on trips to Africa until 2011 and remains an avid Zoo ambassador, Cathryn wrapped up a remarkable stint as the Zoo's beloved cat ambassador during the tenure of current Zoo Director—and Cathryn's good friend—Thane Maynard.

She worked closely with and became dear friends with many people over the years, but especially her *compadres* Kris Kalnow and Gary Denzler. The Maier family, former owners of Frisch's Restaurants, were steadfast supporters of Cathryn's outreach and education work. Cathryn met and dazzled celebrities including Prince Charles, the Cincinnati Bengals, and the Namibian Ambassador to the United States, accompanied by the cheetahs Angel, Kenya, Moya, and Sarah, her performing and life partners.

🐾 Cathryn Hilker and Thane Maynard

The cats are coming. I promise. But in keeping with Cathryn's life mantra that "your life is defined by the people you meet," this chapter celebrates a special set of influencers and partners and the wonderful stories they created together.

—∞ Cathryn's Early Years at the Zoo ∞—

In the previous chapter, Cathryn's 1962 experience raising Toughy the Tiger on her Mason farm—thanks to Zoo Director Bill Hoff (1961–67)—launched the emergence of her deep relationship with the Cincinnati Zoo. There wasn't much time for volunteering during the next few years, however. Cathryn taught English in both Mason Public Schools and The Seven Hills School (then Hillsdale) from 1963–65, married Carl "Hege" Hilker, Jr., in 1969, and had a son, Carl Hilker III, in 1970.

Ed Maruska succeeded Bill Hoff as Zoo Director in 1968.[37] Both Cathryn and Ed remember a pivotal moment when Cathryn's intense love of cheetahs quietly morphed into a persistent campaign to deepen the Zoo's commitment to the endangered cat.

Maruska had invited Canadian Al Oeming to Cincinnati in 1972 for a wildlife show. Oeming was a former professional wrestler whose fight-name

Answering the Call of the Wild
The Remarkable Life of Cathryn Hosea Hilker

was "Nature Boy," a nod to his boyhood pastime of raising falcons and to his degrees in ornithology and zoology. Oeming left wrestling in 1958 to establish the Alberta Game Farm when he was just 33 years old. By the 1970s, the 500-acre game farm had become a world-renowned facility, a veritable Noah's Ark, believed at the time to be the world's largest collection of exotic wild animals.[38]

From the start of his animal adventure, Oeming had a pet cheetah named Tawana who toured with him in the 1950s doing wildlife shows across Canada. At the time, Tawana was believed to be the only cheetah in Canada.

Cathryn remembers Oeming's invitational visit to Cincinnati as inspiring and amusing:[39] "Oeming came down here from Canada with his cheetah. I was sitting on the end seat at the Zoo's outdoor amphitheater. When Oeming walked in, out of the corner of my eye I saw this cheetah walking down the aisle. As the animal passed me, I saw the look in its eyes. I saw its shoulders so high, the regal movement of the whole cat, just this marvelous creation. I thought I was going to die right there on the spot. It was the first time I ever saw a cheetah that close. I will never forget that memory. I can still feel the thrill today."

One of the stories that Oeming told during his talk was something that happened on the long drive from Canada to Cincinnati. It was reported by the *Cincinnati Enquirer*[40] and elaborated by Cathryn:

He said the cat became restless, and he knew the cheetah well enough to know that he needed to stop for a break. He pulled off the road—there were no super-highways at that time—so the cat could do its business. Then, just as the cat was getting back into the van, a motorcycle zoomed by. The cat took off like a bat out of hell, chasing the motorcycle down the road. Oeming jumped in the van, hoping to catch the cat before the motorcycle got to a policeman and the cat got shot. He found the cat lying in the middle of the road, completely exhausted after the chase. Oeming put the cat in the van and just kept driving. He saw the motorcycle guy and a policeman pass him going the other way, so he held the cat down until they were out of sight.

By 1974, married with a three-year-old son, Cathryn was ready and able to begin active volunteering at the Zoo. Mort (Mrs. Frank) Gusweiler was one of only five women on the Zoo's 26-member Board of Directors. According to a paper written by public relations guru Oliver "Muff" Gale,[41] "some four hundred volunteers, mostly women, were taking part in a variety of activities for the Zoo, principally the Membership campaign. Mrs. Gusweiler's small army of women were working toward a goal of 30,000 members which would produce more than $100,000 annually to support the Zoo." As Cathryn remembers the situation, "we had to go around giving talks about the Zoo with a terrible little promotional film. Somehow it worked!"

She didn't pursue the public relations effort for very long, however. She had to answer the call of the wild. "I became more and more interested in what the Zoo was doing."[42]

— ✸ Innovation in Outreach and Education ✸—

Al Oeming wasn't the only one trying to educate the public about wild animals. Ed Maruska's invitation to Oeming was calculated to help him advance a strategy that was central to the purpose of a modern zoo. Maruska may not have recognized it at the time, but Cathryn would become central to his strategy as well.

Education has always been part of the Cincinnati Zoo's mission, especially for children. As early as 1896, the Zoo formed a partnership with Cincinnati Public Schools to bring children to the Zoo. The complete story of the Cincinnati Zoo's founding and early years is told quite well in a 1993 publication written by David Ehrlinger,[43] and so will not be retold here. But suffice to say for an introduction to this era of innovation, the Cincinnati Zoo had experienced good times and bad from its founding until the 1960s when the trend line of progress began to move up consistently.

During the Bill Hoff era, in 1965 the Zoo launched a formal "School Days" program which "included pre-visit preparation in the classroom, structured tours to emphasize certain themes regarding the animal world, and follow-up studies for classroom use. Volunteers, mostly women, trained as tour guides, were brought into the program and, the schools agreed, these school visits became not only joyous days for the children but a meaningful educational experience.[44] Following closely on the heels of a successful Zoo-sponsored expedition piloted the previous year, the school program was the second plank of the Zoo's efforts to create innovative educational programming.

Maruska remembers vividly the early days at zoos when most of them offered popular circus-like performances, when a zoo was "a bad blend of a prison and a circus."[45] According to Maruska, "the Cincinnati Zoo did some of that, though not to such an extreme. Most zoo shows at the time were undignified animal caricatures. Cats, elephants, ponies, chimps—they wore little hats and pranced around an arena. It wasn't natural behavior, but it was entertaining and popular. How do you transition away from that?"

Over time, Maruska replaced the circus shows with educational programs. Along with developing natural habitats, education was the major focus for the Cincinnati Zoo during Maruska's tenure as director. Determined to extend Hoff's foundational work to recapture the Zoo's early leadership in outreach and education, Ed Maruska led Cincinnati to establish one of the first formal education programs in the country. Zoo supporter Craig Maier, former CEO of Frisch's Restaurants, says that "Ed Maruska was really the leader that made the Zoo what it has become today."

Barry Wakeman, who had been hired in 1968 as a Zoologist, became the Zoo's first education director in 1974, a position he held until he retired in 1993. Thane Maynard, who joined the Zoo's education department in 1977 and later succeeded Wakeman as Education Director, says "we opened the world's first zoo education center with five classrooms, a high school program, and many other programs."

According to Cathryn, Barry Wakeman was "an extraordinary guy. He turned zoo education into a thing of great depth. He influenced me tremendously. His approach was so unique that the Zoo created the education department around him. Part of his approach was to bring small animals such as possums, skunks, and snakes out of the Zoo and into the classroom. The program was called PAT: People and Animals Together."[46]

The 1970s and 1980s were a time of significant advancement in education programming and community outreach:

The importance of education in zoos expanded as worldwide threats to wilderness and wildlife grew and the environmental movement developed. Education and its place in conservation has become a critical role for modern zoos. Through the 1980s the Cincinnati Zoo's Education Department developed in size and in scope, creating awareness, providing information, and encouraging involvement. A variety of school, pre-school, and scout programs emerged, integrated by themes of the diversity and interdependence of life.[47]

Cathryn was key to the Zoo's community outreach and education effort. "Around 1980, I went to Barry and suggested adding a cheetah to do our educational work. Instead of throwing up his hands and screaming, he helped me to achieve that."[48] Cheetahs are tractable—relatively easy to handle—and quickly became the stars of the Zoo's shows. According to Cathryn, "there was something magical about seeing an animal with no bars, about an animal walking quietly by a trainer's side and getting up on a seat or a table to get a treat while the trainer explains what she is doing. I used to get wonderful letters from children, and it became a popular program."

Advancing the growth and development of a cheetah program wasn't always a smooth process. Ed Maruska had definite views about how the Zoo's education programs should evolve, which occasionally put him at odds with Cathryn Hilker and her cat partner, Kris Kalnow. As Cathryn describes the situation:

Ed threw me out of his office when I said I wanted to start a full-blown cheetah program. He said, 'Who the hell do you think you are?' I told him I just thought it would be a good idea. He responded, 'You'll never have a cheetah program as long as I'm the Zoo Director, so get the hell out.' I mean, he threw me out of his office. So I called Kris Kalnow. She was drop-dead gorgeous, and by God I used that to my advantage. By the time I left Ed's office with Kris, all he said was this: 'I want you to understand. I will give you permission to do this, but don't ever ask me for any help. I will not give you any money. I will not support you in any way. If this is what you two want to do, you do it.' Well, that's exactly what we wanted to hear. We raised the money.

Explaining why he initially denied Cathryn's request, Maruska points out that the zoo field was not in complete agreement about using animals for educational purposes at that time, particularly if there was any direct contact with people. "I was reminded of animals being trotted out like a carnival show, which in many ways was cruel. But then I began to see that those animals, and the people working with them, were ambassadors."

Cathryn made a habit of pitching ideas to Ed Maruska with her ace partner Kris Kalnow who tells this story about one of their schemes.

After we started what became known as the Cat Ambassador Program, we had to go back to Ed and tell him that we needed a place to house the cats. We couldn't continue to keep all of them at home. He agreed to let us create a space for the cats in the basement of the old vacant elephant house. Once again, he told us that we would have to raise the money ourselves because of the Zoo's budget constraints. And so we did it again.

Well, nobody had used the elephant house in years. It was disgusting! For days on end, our cat trainer consultant and I were taking years of decomposed elephant poop out of the building. Every once in a while, Cathryn would come down to the basement to inquire 'are you doing okay?' We were ready to bop her. After we finally got the floors cleaned, we discovered that the walls were in terrible shape. And even though we didn't exactly know what we were doing, we dry-walled and painted the entire basement. It looked beautiful!

The night we completed the finishing touches, we brought our first tiger to the new space. Cathryn and I were convinced that the tiger should not be alone on its first night, so we made a bed of straw and spent the night with the tiger. And then the sweetest thing happened. At 7:00 am, Thane Maynard brought two goodie bags of PB&J sandwiches so we would have something to eat when we woke up in the morning.

Well, as soon as the new space was finished, Ed declared it to be so beautiful that it needed to be used for a different purpose. He gave it to Gary Denzler, who we dearly love, to use for his bird shows. It became his building and not ours. So back to the drawing board—I

🐾 Top: Cathryn and Angel at GCF with (L-R) Bill Bahlman, Herb Brown, Carolyn McCoy, Jake Davis, and Bob Westheimer; Below: GCF Van

still had cats at home, and Cathryn still had Carrie Cougar and Angel at her farm.

Initially, Cathryn was using her own car to transport the cats back and forth from home to the Zoo and to schools. As the program grew in popularity, so did the need to consider purchasing a larger (and safer) vehicle. The Zoo didn't have the money to buy a van, so Cathryn asked the Greater Cincinnati Foundation (GCF) for funding. Kris Kalnow said, "With Angel staring at them from atop a conference table, needless to say, they said yes!"

Answering the Call of the Wild
The Remarkable Life of Cathryn Hosea Hilker

Carolyn McCoy, who was GCF's director at the time, says "the story about that day is a funny one. Cathryn and I had arranged for Angel to come with her to the office, but no one else knew it! The phone call from the downstairs guard (in the downtown U.S. Bank building) went something like this: 'Ma'am, there is a woman down here from the Zoo with a big cat who says you are expecting her.' We always joked about the grant request interview, saying, 'After Angel jumped up on the table, laid down and started swishing her tail, everyone agreed: let's get the checkbook.' What's even funnier is that we didn't actually write checks!"

The resource-sharing story continues from Kris Kalnow. "But guess what? We had to share the van for transportation to shows, as well as the building, with Gary Denzler's birds. Let's just say that there was a bit of chaos with cats smelling the scent of birds and batting remnant bird feathers all around the van."

—∞ Cathryn's Champions: Ed Maruska and Thane Maynard ∞—

Over time, Ed Maruska became Cathryn's greatest champion. Thane Maynard attributes the outreach program's success to Cathryn's natural ease of connection with people. "It became the Cat Ambassador Program from day one. The Zoo's reputation from 1980 until baby hippo Fiona came on the scene in 2017 was formed in part by the cheetahs."

Ed Maruska, Zoo Director 1968-2000 [49]

The collection has always been our core, our reason for being. But we needed to build year-round programs as diversified as the animal collection to gain community support.[50] —*Ed Maruska*

Ed Maruska always knew he wanted to work with animals. "As far back as I can remember, I had an inherent interest in animals and wild things. My aunt related a story where she took me to the Brookfield Zoo (now the Chicago Zoological Park) at seven years old and couldn't get me out."

Maruska started his career at the Lincoln Park Zoo in Chicago, working his way up to head keeper. He got a job there by answering an ad in the *Chicago Tribune* for a reptile keeper.

Cincinnati Zoo Director Bill Hoff brought Maruska down from Chicago in 1962 to be the general curator. Maruska ran zoo operations while Hoff was out raising money. "At that time, it was more of a farmyard than it was a zoo. It was held together with bubblegum and duct tape." But it had some interesting animals, including a collection of cats and a rhino.

When Maruska became Zoo Director in 1968 at age 34, he was one of the country's youngest zoo directors. He had an ambitious and transformative vision of zoo excellence. It didn't include cute circus acts or animals in cages. But it did include education programs on site at the Zoo.

Ed Maruska (1968)

What he could not see clearly at the beginning was how a community outreach program—Cathryn Hilker's contribution to the Zoo's vision—would help to increase attendance. It took some time for her to convince him, some would say to wear him down, until he finally said "yes." Going out into the community could be an educational and outreach strategy designed to bring people into the Zoo.

In the 1960s, the Zoo's annual attendance was about 250-300,000 people a year. (Today it is over 1.2 million annually.) There was little community or financial support, and few paid employees. As a result, the Cincinnati Zoo was run down. "I decided to develop a volunteer program, a corps of ambassadors working at the Zoo and as a speaker's bureau out in the community. They helped build Zoo attendance, which caught the attention of city officials when they saw how bad things were."

Under Ed's leadership, the Zoo launched a major park revitalization program. The transition from old-style bar-enclosed cages to open grottoes and display areas had begun in the 1930s, a move in which Cincinnati was a pioneer. But Maruska took it to another level with a $10 million plan for facilities and landscaping that included space for formal education programs. He also secured a Hamilton County tax levy in 1982 to support Zoo operations after Cincinnati had led the way in the Ohio legislature to permit this new source of revenue.

"The purpose of the Zoo wasn't just to come look at animals. Visitors needed to be aware of the plight of wild animals and conservation measures. Eventually we were able to display the animals more appropriately in the park. Zoos around the country have emulated Cincinnati's education program. I am so proud of the Zoo and how it is still progressing and improving."

Maruska's generation defined what modern zoos are all about: conservation, recreation, education, and research. In a 2017 story about Maruska, *zoophoria. net* shared this accolade: "Ed Maruska has been regarded as one of the classic silverback directors of the zoo field. In a career that spanned nearly four decades, he led the Cincinnati Zoo to being one of the premier institutions in the country and helped establish breeding programs for endangered species within zoos. Maruska made several innovations during his tenure including opening the first insect exhibit at an American zoo and integrating gorillas in family groups. Although he has been retired since 2001, he remains a legend in the field."

According to Ed, "My legacy is taking a failing institution, which it was at the time, and turning that into a world-class institution that continues to excel. I built a base that's hit some bars that will be pretty hard to lower. I set them high. When you've got action and animals behaving naturally, you have greater visitor appreciation. It's a world we share with animals and, as humans, we need that."

Thane Maynard, Zoo Director 2007 to present
Be joyful though you have considered all the facts. —Wendell Berry

Thane Maynard's official bio on the Cincinnati Zoo's website offers a glimpse of the traditional points one might expect to know about the leader of an important community institution: where he grew up (Florida), where he went to college (Rollins), where he got a masters' degree (University of Michigan School of Natural Resources), what he studied (the environment and wildlife ecology), how many books he's published (over a dozen), and a bit about how his resonant voice has made him a celebrity at home and beyond (the nationally syndicated radio program "The 90-Second Naturalist" which Maynard authors and delivers).

Maynard has become the personification of the Cincinnati Zoo, internationally known for his dedication to wildlife preservation, research, and education. He has even been recognized (in 2012) as a Maasai elder in a small village in Kenya to honor his work there on wildlife conservation.

Thane Maynard (1986)

Maynard's illustrious career at the Cincinnati Zoo spans more than 40 years (minus a short gap during 2000-01 as executive director of a 255-acre outdoor education center in Seattle). He joined the Zoo's nascent education group in 1977, became the director of education in 1993, and was named Zoo Director in 2007.

But all those facts merely scratch the surface of Maynard's passion for biodiversity, commitment to conservation, and the magnetic influence he has had on the Cincinnati Zoo. His vision is to inspire every visitor with wildlife every day.

"Thane's a very motivating guy, and that rubs off on everybody," said Gary Denzler in a 2013 *Cincinnati Magazine* feature. "The whole community has embraced him. He's the kind of guy, when you walk into work every day, you just want to keep going forward, improving on things. And Thane may be the public face of the zoo, but he doesn't make it about himself."

He shares that innate sense of humility with Cathryn Hilker. Maynard and Cathryn have been colleagues and dear friends for more than 40 years. She was already working at the Zoo in 1977 when Maynard joined the education department. They have journeyed a long and winding road together to create a window on the wild for thousands of people inside the Zoo, in Cincinnati, and in Africa. Together they have helped to set new standards for modern zoos that have been replicated and emulated all over the world.

🐾 Thane and Cathryn with baby white tigers.

Three additional traits shared by Thane and Cathryn are voracious reading habits, an amazing ability to remember facts and snippets of artful writing, and the engaging ability to tell a good story to any size audience. Cathryn describes him as "romantic about the natural world with the soul of a poet. He reads everywhere. Leaning against a pillar in an airport. Standing in line. On a plane. In the back of a taxi."[51]

That same notion is echoed by former director Ed Maruska: "With his cub-scout good looks and rapid-fire delivery, Maynard is the ideal public speaker. It doesn't take much to get him on a roll because he carries around an incredible amount of information in his head."[52] A 2013 feature in *Cincinnati Magazine* amplifies the importance and durability of storytelling: "Wherever you might see him, he's bound to be surrounded by people who can't seem to get enough of his stories. Nothing seems beyond the realm of possibility to Thane Maynard, and his stories are testament to his perpetual optimism."[53]

Cathryn is certain that the Zoo's Cat Ambassador Program would never have evolved into the robust set of programs it represents today without Maynard's leadership. He was willing to take a chance, zero in on a mission, and engage everyone to share the journey. "He's a visionary. I look at Thane as a harbinger of things to come."

As you might expect from this lead-in, Maynard could tell a zillion stories about Cathryn spanning their 40-plus year friendship. When asked to apply his laser focus to narrowing down huge possibilities to the most fun stories, Thane settled on two travel adventures in New York. This telling, attributed to Thane, includes bits of color commentary blended from several sources because these stories were also the favorites of others who know them both well.

Cathryn is an extremely prudent woman. There's nothing racy about her at all. We were invited to New York to attend the 2006 Explorers Club award ceremony where Mike Fay[54] was to be honored with the prestigious Explorers Club Medal. We were staying at the Waldorf Astoria. As we were checking in, Cathryn told the guy at the desk that we would be sharing a room. He gave me a look like, 'Hey, it's a fancy hotel and older ladies bring in young guys all the time.' Well Cathryn caught the look and said 'Don't you give him that look, that is not what this is about. We want separate beds, young man.' For a minute, they thought you were my girlfriend, my 'Cougar Cathryn.'

Cathryn and Thane

On an earlier trip to New York in the mid-1990s, Cathryn and I traveled with Kenya the cheetah and a tiger to appear on *Good Morning America*. It wasn't easy to do at that time, but we convinced the bureaucratic city-owned Bronx Zoo to let us bring the animals there to stay overnight. Then came the question of where Cathryn and I would stay. Our hotel option was to stay at the Mayflower, which was long past its glory days. At the time, the Zoo's budget was tight and we were cheap, so instead of a hotel we slept on the floor at my sister-in-law Shayla Stewart's apartment on West 110th. I mean, what kind of a plan was that? Today we would have somebody pick us and the animals up at the airport and we would stay in a proper hotel.

Shayla borrowed a beat-up windowless van for us to transport the animals from the Bronx Zoo into Manhattan for the show. We had to get there very early. As we're crossing through Harlem headed for Midtown, we ended up in a fender bender. Imagine the scene, with two large cats, me, Cathryn, and my sister-in-law. I was terrified! Imagine the liability and publicity. But Cathryn gets out of the van, chats with the other people involved, and everything was fine. They had a beat-up car, and we had a beat-up van, so nobody cared about a few more dents.

──❧ *Forever Friends:* ❧── *Gary Denzler, the Maier Family, and Kris Kalnow*

Gary Denzler the "Bird Man"

We had so much fun together. I felt very lucky to have a friend like Cathryn. In all our years together, we never had a harsh word to say. I supported her and she supported me. —Gary Denzler

Gary Denzler started working at the Zoo in 1967 just as Bill Hoff was departing for the director's job at the St. Louis Zoo and Ed Maruska was

🐾 Gary Denzler

transitioning into the Cincinnati director role. Except for a four-year stint in the Navy during the Viet Nam War (1969–73), Gary worked at the Zoo for 40 years until his retirement in 2017. He spent most of those years as the director of the Zoo's bird show.

He was destined to be a "bird man" from the age of 12 when a bird landed and perched on his hand. He was smitten, particularly with falcons and hawks.

Gary and Cathryn were trailblazers, innovators of a new era of Zoo education under Ed Maruska's leadership as Zoo director and Barry Wakeman's guidance as education director. They were pioneers in establishing formal education programs.

According to Gary, "What Cathryn was doing was totally unique. There were other bird shows around the country, but no cheetahs. I have always admired Cathryn for her passion to save the cheetah, beyond the show, for her work in Namibia. I was doing a dream job, one that I always wanted to do. But I got paid and supported my family. Both Kris and Cathryn did it every day—even if it was nearly 100 degrees and we were all sweating to death—because they loved those cats so much. We touched many people in our lives with the animals we love."

There was a certain kinship between the animals as well. "Falcons and cheetahs are each the fastest in their respective categories in the animal kingdom. They both have malar stripes on their faces to keep out the sun. And they both have to eat fast because they are not the top predators."

Cathryn and Gary were aligned with Ed Maruska on his goal of transforming the Zoo's relationship to the community. No more circus acts! Let the animals do what they are designed to do, in the case of cheetahs to run! "An animal in captivity that never does anything isn't in a great situation. Studies conducted by the Center for Conservation and Research of Endangered Wildlife (CREW) at the Cincinnati Zoo showed that animals with the lowest levels of cortisol (a symptom of stress) were the animals from Cathryn's show. They were active, not sitting in cages being watched by visitors."

Nearly all modern Zoo animals are born in captivity. For many animals, including cheetahs, living in the wild is not a great life! Gary finds that these lines from the movie *Madagascar* sum up the situation completely:

Marty the Zebra asks the penguins, "What are you guys doing?"

Private the Penguin replies, "We're digging to Antarctica!"

Skipper the Penguin goes on to say, "We're going to the wide-open spaces!
To the wild."

Upon landing in Antarctica, the penguins are buffeted by wind and surrounded
by a big mound of snow.

Skipper says, "Well this sucks."

When Gregg Hudson took over as Zoo director in 2001, he accelerated and augmented the campus master plan developed under Maruska's tenure. During Hudson's six years as director, one of the greatest advancements from Gary's perspective was a new amphitheater and stage built entirely for his bird show. The old stage had been shared by Gary for birds, Cathryn for cats, and Cecil Jackson for elephants. After a new elephant house was built, each animal show was able to offer educational opportunities in its own designated space. There were additional advancements under Hudson's leadership that elevated the Zoo's commitment to cheetahs. In 2005, the Zoo unveiled a $6 million, 3-acre area just for cheetahs designed by architect Gary Hang Lee, and in 2007, a new cheetah run opened to the public.

One of Thane Maynard's favorite stories about Cathryn and Gary was the duo's sturdy relationship. They worked together every day for years, sharing the same stage, typically doing two shows a day. "Probably a decade into the cat show, in a good brotherly way, Gary teased Cathryn by saying that her show was boring just jumping her cat with a leash. 'You need to run that cheetah,' Gary said."

Gary claims this as one of his favorite stories as well, picking up where Thane left off. One day, when Gary was at Cathryn's farm during a cheetah run, he put his ear to the ground as the cheetah raced by. He could hear the cheetah's claws digging into the earth as the animal sped toward its target. With a vision of creating that experience at the Zoo, and an idea of a possible location on campus, he paced off 100 yards across a parking lot and made a proposal to transform that space. Thus the Cheetah Run was born.

The Maier Family and Frisch's Sponsorship

I owe Frisch's a great debt for my career at the Zoo. —Cathryn Hilker

"Cathryn would call. We would write a check. Cathryn would call. We would write a check. When Cathryn said she was going to do something, she did it! You fell in love with her immediately. If Cathryn asked for something for the Zoo, we wrote a check. It was that simple."[55]

This pattern, this wonderful relationship, started around 1974 when Cathryn was first working as a volunteer on the Zoo's outreach and education programs. Cathryn knew Jack Maier because she showed horses with him. In addition to owning Frisch's Restaurants, Maier was president of the Greater Cincinnati charity horse show for several years. "So I wrote him a letter one time, proposing that we take animals into more schools. I needed money for posters, brochures, and gas because we were using our own cars to transport the animals. He called and said 'I would love to do that. We will sponsor that program.' So that's how it all started. They sponsored the Frisch's Wildlife Center, Frisch's Discovery Center, the Animal Recreation Center, the Cheetah Run, outreach programs, vans. They were so generous!"

There's no question that the relationship was mutually beneficial—a stellar example of social marketing just as the novel concept was being introduced to the nonprofit sector in the 1970s. Cathryn says, "We always thanked them in public, and I think the Maiers really liked the fact that this was a good PR program for them. Jack told me one time that we gave him the best product per dollar compared to any advertising he ever did. We would get letters from kids saying things like, 'We're going to eat at Frisch's on Friday night because you brought the cats to our school.' That was really neat!" Jack had Cathryn make little plaques for the sides of the cat carriers, and the staff wore patches on their Safari shirts that said Frisch's Discovery Center.

When Jack Maier passed away in 2005, two of his children, Craig and Karen—executives in the Frisch's company—stepped right into the relationship for a decade until they sold the business in 2015. Company sponsorship from the new owners continues to this day.

Craig Maier says that "she changed the world for cheetahs. You can always say there are cheetahs in the world because of Cathryn. Who would think that

🐾 Left: Frisch's Wildlife Theater; Right: Frisch's Discovery Center

you come from Cincinnati, Ohio, and that you do something about changing the future for the fastest animal on the face of the earth? It's pretty remarkable."

Kris Kalnow and the Beginnings of the Cat Ambassador Program[56]

Two crazy ladies at the Zoo: here they come, there they go!

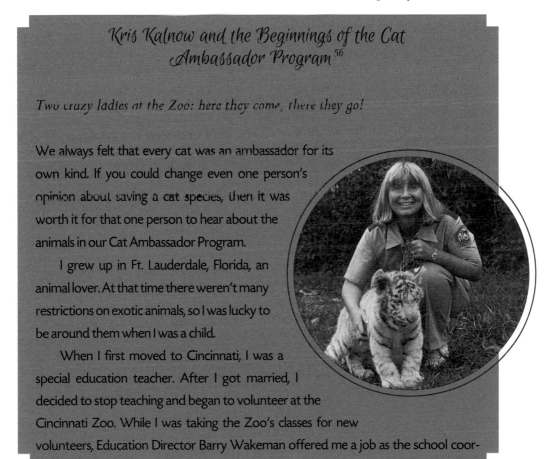

We always felt that every cat was an ambassador for its own kind. If you could change even one person's opinion about saving a cat species, then it was worth it for that one person to hear about the animals in our Cat Ambassador Program.

I grew up in Ft. Lauderdale, Florida, an animal lover. At that time there weren't many restrictions on exotic animals, so I was lucky to be around them when I was a child.

When I first moved to Cincinnati, I was a special education teacher. After I got married, I decided to stop teaching and began to volunteer at the Cincinnati Zoo. While I was taking the Zoo's classes for new volunteers, Education Director Barry Wakeman offered me a job as the school coordinator to schedule teachers' visits to the Zoo. I got to take the animals home to see if they would be 'pet friendly' with the kids. I had all kinds of crazy animals at my house.

Cathryn with Carrie Cougar

I first started working at the Zoo in 1982. My desk was right across from Cathryn's. She was panicking at the time because the Zoo had given her a green light to start a cat ambassador program, but she didn't have the cats. Because I was also in charge of acquiring animals for the education department, I offered to help Cathryn.

One of the people I called offered us a cougar for free because she was the runt of the litter. When the cougar arrived at the airport she was in a carrier no larger than a shoe box! It was tiny, and frankly pathetic looking. I instantly got on my 'high horse' and proclaimed her to be the most beautiful animal we have at the Zoo.

As we began to add cats in anticipation of the new program, we ran into a problem because there was not enough space for them to live at the Zoo. Angel and Carrie Cougar already lived with Cathryn at her farm in Mason, so I agreed to host Missy the serval and Mr. Spock the caracal at my home. I built a room onto our house for the cats that at one point included the Zoo's white tigers.

Neither Cathryn nor I had ever trained cats. It's not something that you just naturally know how to do. But that didn't stop us.

The Zoo's bird trainer at the time, Steve Martin, connected us with a young woman in San Diego, Jaye Apperson, who was an exotic animal trainer and consultant. Jaye's specialty was training bears for movies and television. We hopped on a plane to visit Jaye and to check out the San Diego Zoo's cat programs. It turned out to be one of the worst weather episodes in California's history, a 'super *el niño*.' As we were driving, the roads were collapsing. And when we arrived at the Zoo, it was closed—something that had never happened before!

When we met Jaye, we discovered that she was tiny—maybe four feet, ten inches—which was quite comedic with six-foot-two Cathryn! Jaye agreed to come to Cincinnati for the summer of 1983 and lived with my husband Cal and me. For three months she taught Cathryn and me how to train cats, and then we were on our own. She came back the following year, this time for five months. She was an incredible trainer!

🐾 "The Bickersons" Kris and Cathryn

Ed Maruska was really keeping a close eye on us. At the time we thought he was just being overbearing, but now we realize that his chief concern was safety–for us and for the cats. We had fun, but we were dead serious. Cathryn and I never gave up our guard with these cats.

Here I need to interject a funny story about Cathryn's down jacket that describes her to a 'T.' She loved that thing. Her mother had repaired it for her many times over the years because she was always ripping it. On our way to a show I said 'Cathryn, we really shouldn't do a cat show with feathers coming out of your coat. It looks like the cats did it, and they're going to be batting the feathers on stage.' So the next day, Cathryn comes to the Zoo, her jacket tears covered with duct tape. Her answer for everything was duct tape–she was so frugal! I said, 'Seriously, Cathryn, you cannot go into these shows with duct tape on your jacket.' Cathryn's retort was, 'Well, Kris, it's a perfectly good coat.' I disagreed, so I bought her a new one and took the other coat away. She loved it!

We were definitely aligned in our passion for the cats, and our approach to outreach and education. But everyone called us 'the Bickersons.' Sometimes people are floored by that, but that's just the tenor of our friendship. It's been that way forever.

We used to go to the Echo Restaurant in Hyde Park every Friday to get a fish sandwich.[57] Even if we had cats with us in the van, we would park on the street and head inside to eat. One day as we were leaving, one of the ladies came up to me to ask 'What is wrong? Do you not like her? I can't believe how you two talk to one another.' She was a little surprised to learn that we were–and are–good friends. Cathryn and I worked together as partners in the cat programs until my third child was born, and we have been 'best friends forever' since then.

"Fat Fish Friday" with Cathryn and Kris at the Echo

Cincinnati Bengals

Stories about Cathryn and other Zoo staffers taking chimpanzees and tigers onto the football field during Bengals' football games are legendary.

In a paper chronicling the history of the Zoo, Oliver Gale wrote this description of the spectacle: "When Beauty the chimpanzee's inspiration faded, her colleague Angel the cheetah took over with similar success. Benzoo, the Bengal tiger chosen as mascot for the Bengals, Cincinnati's professional football team, so thoroughly enjoyed her Sunday outings to the stadium that she would pace impatiently in her cage as the hour approached, and leap without prodding into the wheeled conveyance that would parade her before fifty thousand fans."[58]

Cathryn and her colleagues had a great run of experiences taking young animals to the Bengals games. They took a young lion for a while, until it got too big. Then they switched to a young tiger. At half time they would go out in the middle of the field. Kris Kalnow was Cathryn's partner for many of their cat journeys to the Bengals' stadium. She recalls:

> You always have to remember that these are exotic animals, and
> you never know when something can snap. Cathryn was good about

🐾 Kris and Cathryn at a Bengals game

enforcing that. We joked and had a good time, but we never took a chance.

But we did have a 'situation.' We had two young white tigers, the first ones that Ed Maruska let us have at home. Cathryn was a nervous wreck because each cat was worth $60,000. Both of them lived at home with me at the time, so I didn't think it was a big deal.

We took them to a Bengals game. All of a sudden, one of the cats races off under the stadium. And, of course, it's the cat Cathryn was managing. I'm not kidding, faster than any military person under attack, she hit the ground and rolled under the stadium to find the cat. Imagine the picture of this six-foot-two person rolling under the stadium. The cat sauntered out before Cathryn could roll back—I just called him and out he came. The entire stadium saw the whole thing! When Cathryn came out from under the stadium, there was roaring applause in the stadium. Cathryn said, 'He's going to kill me, how am I going to explain this to Ed Maruska?'

U.S. Ambassador from Namibia, Leonard N. Iipumbu

The Hamilton County Board of Commissioners declared May 2, 2002, "Leonard N. Iipumbu Day" in honor of the Namibian Ambassador's visit to the United States. Ambassador Iipumbu also received a key to the City of Cincinnati. According to Thane Maynard, "he was a charming man, right out of central casting, stuffed into a Western suit."

Establishing a strong partnership with Namibia was quite natural because of the Zoo's relationship with the Cheetah Conservation Fund. Cincinnati Zoo was one of the first American zoos to successfully breed cheetahs (in 1974). Both special recognitions expressed Cincinnati's gratitude to Namibia for the gift of four orphaned cheetahs from the country's then-president, Dr. Sam Nujoma. This was an important gift because these cheetahs were born in the wild, expanding the pool of cheetahs beyond those bred and born in captivity. The Cincinnati Zoo kept two and donated two to other zoos.

During his two-day visit, Ambassador Iipumbu spent time at the Cincinnati Zoo to see the cheetahs' new habitat, declaring, "I am delighted to see the cheetahs in their new spacious home and see the wonderful care they

🐾 Top: (L-R) Ambassador Leonard Iipumbu, City Council Member Minette Cooper, and Hamilton County Commissioner Todd Portune; Below: Cathryn Meets Prince Charles in Palm Beach (1988)

are receiving. These animals would have (otherwise) died."[59] Cathryn Hilker hosted Ambassador Iipumbu at her Mason farm. "He stood in the rain to watch Sahara demonstrate her running ability as she raced down the field and skidded to a stop at his feet! He said the rain was a blessing because it hardly ever rains in Namibia."[60]

Charles, Prince of Wales

In March 1998, Prince Charles visited Palm Beach, Florida, to play polo and help raise money for the Maasai Mara game preserve in Kenya. Jim Fowler, co-host of the television show *Wild Kingdom*, was there to create an animal show. Cathryn and Cincinnati Zoo staff member Mike Dulaney drove from Cincinnati to join him with an aardvark named Ivanhoe and her cheetah Angel in tow. After Fowler startled the Prince by sending an African tawny eagle to deliver a message of thanks, Cathryn joined the show with a carsick cheetah. Angel still knew how to perform, though: when the Prince leaned forward to pet her, the *Broward Sun-Sentinel* reported that the cat licked his hand.[61]

Siegfried & Roy

Entertainers, magicians, and big-cat stars of stage and television Siegfried & Roy are practically household names. Siegfried Fischbacher and Roy Horn performed with white tigers and lions for thirteen years, from 1990 until 2003, when their career was tragically ended by an accident on stage.

The Cincinnati Zoo had an important relationship with Siegfried & Roy. During the heyday of their career in 1998, the performers loaned two white tigers named Sunshine and Future to the Zoo. Later that year they gave a hand-raised white lion cub named Prosperity to the Cincinnati Zoo to assimilate with other lions. This gift resulted in four cubs being born, three of which were shared with the Toledo Zoo. Prosperity recently died (January 2020) at the age of 22. Her daughter Gracious, still living at the Zoo, is 18 years old.

🐾 (L-R) Elissa Knights, Roy Horn, Siegfried Fischbacher, and Cathryn Hilker

Baby cheetahs in Namibia, courtesy of Cheetah Conservation Fund

5

Passion for Saving the Cheetah, an Endangered Species

———❦———

Problem-solving becomes a very real thing when you move from the heart of what you love to the reality of what you must do. I stopped everything to pursue the cheetah.[62] —*Cathryn Hilker*

When Cathryn was only a young child, she developed a deep affinity for cheetahs. She saw them at the Cincinnati Zoo. She imagined them as she daydreamed at home on the farm while gazing upon her parents' exotic lamp depicting a world of wild animals. She dreamt about them. Especially their eyes. She was captivated by this window into their living souls. And she was mesmerized by the cheetah's graceful gait, so much like that of her beloved horses, so much like her own forbearance. In her forties, when Cathryn started volunteering (and eventually working) at the Cincinnati Zoo, her resolve to activate cheetah conservation snapped into focus when then-director Ed Maruska invited Canadian Al Oeming and his pet cheetah to visit Cincinnati.

Cathryn's story wouldn't be complete without a bit of education about cheetahs and their current state in a fragile wildlife ecosystem.

———❦ *Endangered Species* ❦———

A few centuries ago, cheetahs roamed from the Indian subcontinent to the shores of the Red Sea and throughout much of Africa. As fleet of foot as they are, though, they couldn't outrun the long reach of humanity.[63]

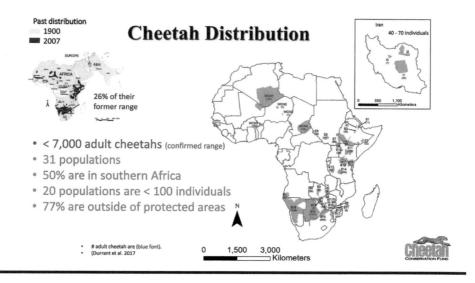

Cheetah Distribution

Past distribution
1900
2007

26% of their former range

Iran
40 - 70 individuals

- **< 7,000 adult cheetahs** (confirmed range)
- **31 populations**
- **50% are in southern Africa**
- **20 populations are < 100 individuals**
- **77% are outside of protected areas**

- # adult cheetah are (blue font).
- (Durrant et al. 2017)

0   1,500   3,000
Kilometers

Cheetahs are a species at risk. In 1900, there were 100,000 cheetahs globally. By 1980, the number of cheetahs had shrunk to 25,000. Ten years later, the number of cheetahs dropped another 50% to 12,500. Although the pace of eradication has slowed, the number of cheetahs is still falling: today there are about 7,100-7,500 cheetahs in the wild and in captivity at zoos.[64] "The largest population in the wild is found in Namibia, primarily on commercial livestock farmlands, and is estimated at 2–3,000 animals."[65]

Cheetahs are members of the *felidae* cat family. Though cheetahs belong to the same family as all other cats, including lions, leopards, and the domestic house cat, they are different in several ways. "If cheetahs seem a breed apart, it's because they are. Not only are they a separate species from the other great cats, but they belong to a separate genus as well, a genus with just one member: themselves."[66] The genus and species name is *Acinonyx jubatus*.

The cheetah is the world's fastest mammal and the most specialized of all 37 cat species. Cheetahs are tall and slender with long, delicate legs, and they can run faster than any other land animal. A cheetah can accelerate to 65 miles per hour and back to zero in a matter of seconds. For comparison, a racehorse can run 45 miles an hour.

Cheetahs are relatively small cats weighing between 60 and 120 pounds, average 2.3–2.6 feet tall, and have an average lifespan of 11 years. A heavy black line that looks like a tear streak, called a malar stripe, absorbs sunlight

Malar stripes

to keep the sun's glare out of its eyes in the cheetah's natural habitat of savanna and dry forest.

The cheetah is built for speed versus power, which is different from other large cats. Its flexible spine, lean body, small head, and specialized organs are all designed for speed. "The cheetah's curious semi-retractable claw is a feature they share with no other cat."[67] Their pads are grooved and hardened like tire treads, and their claws stick out like a dog's nails. The cheetah grips the ground during high-speed acceleration, pursuit, and screeching to a halt. Its powerful tail works like a rudder, supporting balance during a zig-zag chase for prey.

The cheetah is further set apart from other large cats by its nonaggressive, shy nature. When challenged by other predators, the cheetah backs away. They are often beaten out by larger, more aggressive wildlife during the chase for food. A cheetah might even give up its captured prey to other animals. Its basic nature and hunting skills are so special that cheetahs have been kept extensively by royalty and the wealthy for pets

Claws and paws

and hunting sports for nearly 5,000 years. These practices, though declining, are contributing factors to the endangerment of the world's cheetah population.

Cheetahs are most prevalent in the grasslands of East Africa, living mostly today in national parks like the Serengeti or Maasai Mara. But they can range throughout any open country if there is adequate prey for them to survive. The largest population of free-ranging cheetah live in Namibia, Africa, but are also found in some parts of Iraq, Iran,

Claws for stopping, rudder tail for balance

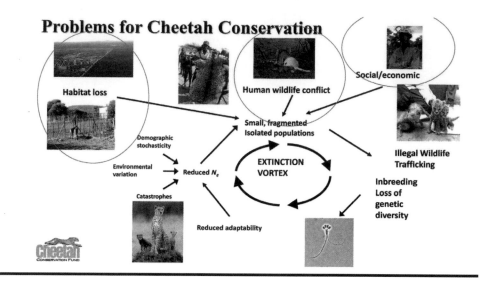

Problems for Cheetah Conservation

Habitat loss

Human wildlife conflict

Social/economic

Demographic stochasticity

Environmental variation

Catastrophes

Reduced N_e

Small, fragmented isolated populations

EXTINCTION VORTEX

Illegal Wildlife Trafficking

Inbreeding Loss of genetic diversity

Reduced adaptability

Cheetah CONSERVATION FUND

and Pakistan. Namibia is a desert country, much like the American Southwest, where cattle and sheep ranching are the primary agricultural pursuits.

According to Dr. Laurie Marker, founder of the Cheetah Conservation Fund (CCF), "We're losing them. The numbers continue to climb, and the big issues are all human issues."

Only one in 10 cheetahs born in the wild makes it to adulthood. Due to a combination of challenging habitat and human factors, "mortality among cubs can run as high as 95 percent. Many female cheetahs go their entire lives without raising a single cub to maturity."[68] A rare few female cheetahs are super-moms, raising multiple litters from different male cheetahs and even fostering the cubs of other females, a natural hedge against extinction in an uncertain environment.

Like all spotted and striped cats, cheetahs have long been under pressure from illegal poaching by the fur trade. Wild cheetahs are sometimes captured for the pet trade, but over-hunting is not the principal problem facing cheetahs. Loss of habitat exacerbated by climate change, conflict and competition with large predators and ranchers, as well as its own loss of genetic variation, are the main causes for the cheetah's population decline. Cheetahs are in direct competition with local ranchers—cheetahs are looking for food, and ranchers are protecting their herds—which makes cheetahs constant targets for trapping and hunting.

Today it is hard to image that just 100 years ago Africa was a wild and open place, with small pockets of human agriculture and development. Cheetahs need a large area in which to live. They must have space to run and to hunt for their food. There is less and less room for cheetahs and their survival needs on the increasingly crowded continent of Africa. When people build fenced farms and cities on what was once free-range land, cheetahs get pushed out. This makes life difficult for both predator and prey. To mitigate this challenge, many African

Pregnant cheetah in the Serengeti

countries have set aside tracts of land as national parks to provide safe areas for cheetahs and other wild animals.

Cheetah Conservation: Leadership by the Cincinnati Zoo

One only needs four things to start a Cat Ambassador Program: collar, leash, cat, and 30 years of your life. —Cathryn Hilker

A history of the Cincinnati Zoo published in 1993 notes the Zoo's long-time emphasis on cheetah conservation: "A fenced cheetah exhibit was opened in 1974 near the Children's Zoo with a simulated African landscape planting. In 1976 a Hagenbeck bird exhibit built in 1934 was converted into another cheetah display. Several cheetah births resulted from the expanded space, and the Cincinnati Zoo became the third U.S. zoo to breed this rare species successfully."[69]

The Cat Ambassador Program (CAP), created by Cathryn Hilker at the Cincinnati Zoo in 1980, today encompasses a broad cluster of conservation and educational programs. Its original purpose was quite specific: visit schools with a leash-trained cheetah and other cats from the Zoo. Cathryn's cheetah Angel,[70] often accompanied by Carrie Cougar, were the stars of these school visits. They

🐾 Cathryn with Angel and Carrie Cougar

would occasionally take young tigers and lions with them on school visits as well.

Soon after the original CAP got started, Cathryn came up with the companion idea of having summer programs at the Zoo. That led to what was first called the Cat Show and today called the Cheetah Encounter. From April to October, Zoo guests can witness cheetahs running and other wild cats demonstrating natural behaviors during the Cheetah Encounter.

After Angel died in 1992, a male cheetah named Kenya took over Angel's role. Initially, Kenya would run at Cathryn's farm. Gary Denzler, a Zoo colleague fondly known as the "bird man," came up with the idea to create a cheetah run on the Zoo grounds.

The Cincinnati Zoo's Lead Cat Trainer Linda Castañeda first met Cathryn in 2005 during a college internship.

Cathryn was sitting in an empty classroom with the cheetah brothers Bravo and Chance. She asked me what I wanted to do with my life, and I said that I wanted to do education programs with cats. She said, 'Well, you will have to come here because no one else does this.' and I replied, 'Well, then you will see me again.' I kept my promise and returned in 2007 when a position became available.

I learned all about cheetahs from Cathryn. She always told me that when she was a child, she read in a book that cheetahs could be extinct by the year 2000. Cathryn could not imagine a world without the majestic cheetah roaming the African savanna. To this day she worries about the wild cheetahs, but I always remind her that 2000 has come and gone and the cheetah remains on this earth, in part because of the work she has done to secure its future. Without Cathryn who knows if the cheetah would still be around.

Today, CAP educates more than 150,000 people a year about the importance of cheetahs and other wild cat predators, all of whom are ambassadors for their respective species.

🐾 Tommy T at the Cincinnati Zoo

The Angel Fund, established in 1992 in memory of Cathryn's cheetah Angel, raises funds to support a variety of the cheetah conservation projects at the Zoo and internationally.[71] Over the years, the Zoo and The Angel Fund have supported and participated in many conservation field-projects, including the Cheetah Conservation Fund and Cheetah Outreach in South Africa. "Through the efforts and resolve of three remarkable women—Cathryn Hilker, Annie Beckhelling and Laurie Marker—the hope is that the wild populations of cheetahs will rebound."[72]

With inspiration and initial financial support from The Angel Fund, the Zoo has become a leader in managed cheetah breeding. Zoo scientists believe that people in the United States must see a cheetah to really understand the animal and its endangered situation. Although cheetahs have not historically bred well in captivity, since 1974 ninety (90) cubs have been born at the Zoo's off-site facility in Clermont County. It is called the Mast Farm, named for the family who donated the land. The Zoo is one of nine breeding centers accredited by the American Zoo Association to help create a sustainable cheetah population and prevent extinction of the world's fastest land animal.

"The endangered cheetah population worldwide has stabilized somewhat because of work at the Cincinnati Zoo's Mast Farm in Clermont County, one of the cornerstones for saving the endangered speedster. Recently, three out of eight cheetah cub litters born in North America were born in Cincinnati. And in 2008, a healthy litter of cubs was born in partnership with the Columbus Zoo, including Tommy T at the Cincinnati Zoo."[73]

In 1981, the Cincinnati Zoo started a research program called the Cincinnati Wildlife Research Federation. A decade later, it was renamed the Lindner Center for Reproduction of Endangered Wildlife (CREW). "Most of the world's nearly 40 wild cat species are threatened to some degree with extinction in nature. The Association of Zoos & Aquariums has established a Species Survival Plans (SSPs) for 17 of *felidae* species. Cathryn often worked with these small cats, especially servals and caracals, in the Cat Ambassador Program."[74]

Each year, in conjunction with Miami University's *Project Dragonfly*, the Cincinnati Zoo leads an international Earth Expeditions graduate course for educators to explore inquiry-based learning and engage in cheetah conservation at Cheetah Conservation Fund headquarters in Namibia.

— ⚬⚬ Caring and Sharing ⚬⚬ —

Partnership with the Cheetah Conservation Fund, Namibia[75]

The Cincinnati Zoo and the Cheetah Conservation Fund (CCF) began a partnership in the 1990s to develop and sustain a progressive conservation program for the endangered cheetah in Namibia. The partnership was built (literally) on 28,000 acres secured by Cathryn and Hege Hilker with the Cincinnati Zoo as a reserve to save cheetahs and for CCF headquarters. A three-part strategy has been effective in slowing the demise of the fastest cat in the world: (1) long-term conservation initiatives throughout the range; (2) better livestock management practices to eliminate the need for ranches to kill so many cheetahs; and (3) conservation education programs for local villagers, ranchers, and school children.

🐾 Cathryn and Dr. Laurie Marker in Namibia

CCF director Dr. Laurie Marker's life-long commitment to protect and conserve cheetahs began over 40 years ago at Wildlife Safari in Winston, Oregon. "There I developed the most successful breeding center for cheetahs in all of North America, and the second most successful in the world."[76] During the mid-1970s, Marker visited Namibia and realized that cheetahs were disappearing there because farmers were killing them to protect their herds of cattle. She knew that Namibia had the largest and potentially sustainable population of free-ranging cheetahs in the world. And she learned that the cheetah's survival depends on a total ecological system of farmland management, prey species management, and habitat stability.

"That's when I first discovered that farmers were killing cheetahs like flies, about 800–900 a year. The farmers had no idea that the cheetah was a valuable endangered species, an amazing animal. It is why I kept coming back. Namibia looked like a place where we could actually make a difference. At that time, Namibia was under an apartheid regime and wasn't really open to the rest of the world. But I kept coming and going, and making more and more friends, including some people with local legitimacy who put me in contact with other farmers."

Her experiences in Namibia inspired her to develop an international guide—a Species Survival Plan, including a management plan for cheetahs in captivity which has since been adopted by the Association of Zoos and Aquariums—but quickly realized that time was slipping by and that she needed to do something immediately to save cheetahs in the wild.

Dr. Marker's early research at Wildlife Safari, conducted in conjunction with the Smithsonian National Zoological Park and the National Cancer Institute, revealed the cheetah's lack of genetic diversity. She headed to Washington D.C. as director of the National Zoo's Center for New Opportunities for Animal Health Sciences. Determined to move to Namibia so she could address the challenges of cheetahs in the wild, she headed to Africa soon after Namibia became independent (February 9, 1990).

Around that time is when I first met Cathryn. I was attending lots of international and national events where we would do fundraising. Before my cheetah Khayame died in 1986, I would put her in a crate and fly around the country doing different events and TV programs. I knew Cathryn had gotten a cheetah because I had the cheetah stud book, so I knew where all the cheetahs were located. I began to turn my travel and speaker requests over to Cathryn and Angel, so initially we knew each other only by phone.

In 1988 I attended a conference at the Cincinnati Zoo where Cathryn, of course, made a presentation. It's where we met in person. Cathryn was heartbroken for me that I had recently lost my cheetah

Answering the Call of the Wild
The Remarkable Life of Cathryn Hosea Hilker

Khayame and asked what I was going to do. I said, 'I'm going to Africa: I know the problems, and now we have to solve them. I must find out why people are killing the cheetah.'

Marker founded the Cheetah Conservation Fund (CCF) in 1990 near Otjiwarongo with her then-husband, fellow researcher and conservationist Daniel Kraus. She realized that she had to put down roots in Namibia for anyone to take her seriously. The CCF vision was, and is today, "To see a world in which cheetah live and flourish in co-existence with people and the environment." The mission of CCF is "To be an international center of excellence concerning cheetah conservation, and multi-disciplinary research and education programs; working with all stakeholders to achieve best practice in conservation and management."[77]

Her crusade zeroed in on the ranchers and creating a rancher-friendly approach. "From the start, I really researched why people were losing livestock from cheetahs and other predators. 240 ranchers participated in my study, which took about two years. What we found was that livestock management practices were the problem." Farmers were indiscriminately shooting cheetahs to protect their livestock. The solution? Provide farmers with livestock guard dogs—Anatolian shepherds, one for herding and one for protection, each trained in its respective role from the young age of eight weeks. Ranchers could keep a wary cheetah away from its herd with the use of guard dogs. This was one of the most important innovations for ranchers.

CCF's education and advocacy work reached ranchers and community members through the CCF Education Centre. Future Farmers of Africa training workshops demonstrated how ranchers could integrate livestock and wildlife management with habitat restoration strategies, making them a powerful source for cheetah conservation.

Cathryn cites this simple, elegant solution as one of the most profound initiatives undertaken by CCF. "These farmers work hard. They didn't really want help from anybody. So here's this attractive newcomer, a woman no less, trying to convince the farmers that she can help make their farms more productive. She says to them, 'Let me give you a dog. I will give you the food, and the dog will protect your stock. You won't have to waste your time trapping cheetahs because they won't come near anything.' She would sit at their dinner tables and talk to them like that. And they began to believe her. She gave them puppies, and by golly, it saved their livestock! She showed them by example, too. She got cattle and raised sheep and goats of her own on the farm. She never killed anything. She just showed them how simple it is."

This is where the Hilkers entered the Cheetah Conservation Fund story. They purchased a total of 28,000 acres in Namibia that became the bulkhead of what has become a sophisticated 100,000-acre compound of facilities, research, and programs. "Hege Hilker flew to Africa in 1995 with the down payment for CCF's first land and current headquarters in Otjiwarongo. The next year he purchased an additional 10,000 acres, which he sold in 2013 to the World Wildlife Fund-Namibia for continued use by CCF."[78] Dr. Marker says that the land purchase allowed CCF to put livestock management techniques into practice and conduct research to show farmers that there are ways to live in harmony with predators. The Hilkers also served on the board of directors during the early years.

Cathryn and Hege with Dr. Laurie Marker

In 2000, CCF dedicated an education center at its Namibian field headquarters in the Hilkers' names. Among those on hand was Namibian President Sam Nujoma. That same year, Nujoma gave ten orphaned cheetahs being held at CCF's sanctuary to the United States, four of which helped start the Cincinnati Zoo's breeding center in Clermont County.[79] "As Ed Maruska said to Dr. Marker on one of her many visits to Cincinnati, 'I consider you a member of my staff. You simply do your work in the field.'"[80]

CCF is also dedicated to increasing general awareness worldwide of the cheetah's endangered status. In 2010, Dr. Marker established International Cheetah Day on December 4th in cooperation with the World Conservation

Union." (December 4 was her cheetah Khayame's birthday.) "It is a way to bring awareness to the plight of the cheetah as Africa's most endangered big cat. The species has reached its tipping point. If we don't act to address this problem now—meaning within the next five to 10 years—there may not be enough left to save the species from extinction. But just as humans have threatened the cheetah, we are also the species with the power to save them. For this, we have reason to hope."

CCF celebrated its 30th anniversary in 2020. Its comprehensive program of cheetah research includes basic research on habitat; scientific research in areas such as population biology, reproductive health, and human impacts; and applied research to develop, test, and promote alternative land management practices. Educational programs disseminated in Namibia and internationally cover topics such as predator conflict resolution, and management of both captive and free-ranging cheetah.

Partnership with Cheetah Outreach in South Africa

Cheetah Outreach is a community-based education program in South Africa that uses ambassador cheetahs in school presentations and conducts teacher workshops. Cheetah Outreach also breeds Anatolian shepherd dogs and places them on South African farms to guard livestock to reduce conflict between farmers and predators.

Annie Beckhelling founded Cheetah Outreach in 1992 in Stellenbosch, South Africa. Before turning full attention to cheetah conservation, she was a fashion designer and model. Her models for designing Cheetah Outreach were the Cheetah Conservation Fund in Namibia and the Cincinnati Zoo's Cat Ambassador Program in the United States.

Beckhelling first got involved in cheetah conservation when she heard about the plight of some young orphan cubs whose mother had been shot. Seeing proof of several key conservation concepts in other countries, she decided that she could also try to make a difference in the fate of cheetahs in South Africa. Five years into her fledgling efforts, in 1997, Spier Wine Estates in Stellenbosch donated a hectare of its premier winegrowing land so that Annie could establish an education center for her outreach programs.

🐾 Cathryn and Annie Beckhelling with Bravo and Chance (2006)

Starting with two male cheetahs, "in the first year alone, Shadow visited more than 50,000 people by traveling to educational facilities, community clubs, hotels, malls, and various public events."[81] Inca's job was to greet the 350,000 people who visited the new center in Stellenbosch. Over time, thousands of sponsored lessons were delivered to people who were learning about their native wildlife for the first time.

Cathryn and Annie Beckhelling had met only briefly at an international conservation meeting in California, clicking immediately as fellow "cat people." When Cathryn's cheetah Kenya died suddenly in 1997 after a short illness, Beckhelling learned of Cathryn's situation "and immediately knew what she needed to do. She was raising three cheetah cubs whose mother had unexpectedly died, and Cathryn needed one that had been bred in captivity."[82] As soon as the cubs were old enough to travel, Annie flew with one-year-old Moya as a gift to Cincinnati.

A commemorative plaque on display at Cheetah Outreach celebrates the relationship between Beckhelling's South African organization and the Cincinnati Zoo. The plaque reads: "Moya was born at Spier September 15,

1997, and hand raised at five weeks of age. Moya was donated in August 1998 to the Angel Fund in Cincinnati, Ohio, USA to help in their education and fundraising efforts for the free ranging African cheetah. Our love travels with Moya and we wish him, Cathryn Hilker and the Angel Fund great success with their efforts." In appreciation, The Angel Fund made grants for several years to help Cheetah Outreach develop programs.

Several years later, Annie visited Cincinnati to check in on Moya and exchange ideas on cheetah outreach and education.

Cathryn and Angel (1980s)

6

A Cheetah Named Angel (1981–1992)

You gave me the green fields of Ohio.
I always felt the soft browns of Africa.
I obeyed your words,
I heard the sounds of the wild.
Your hands touched my face,
I felt the winds of my native land.
I walked quietly by your side,
I ran swiftly in my dreams.
You looked into my eyes,
I saw beyond your thoughts.
I allowed you a glimpse into the wild,
You must share what I so freely gave.
"From Angel" —a poem by Cathryn Hilker, 1992

"As she and Angel stand side by side, they look like mother and daughter. Long, graceful, aristocratic, golden hair gleaming in the sun, cool reserved eyes that tell of an iron will, and a wildness within."[84]

With permission from Cathryn Hilker and the Cincinnati Zoo, this chapter of Cathryn's life is best told as a condensed and lightly edited version of her book written to honor Angel's profound influence on cheetah conservation.[83]

In her introduction to the book, Cathryn asserts that, "All animals are important to our world because they are part of the 'web of life.' Just as individual threads of a spider web are connected and are needed to make the web hold together, all life on earth is connected to make the earth strong. All life depends on other forms of life to survive."

—◦◦◦ *The Beginning* ◦◦◦—

In 1981 two female cheetah cubs were born at the Columbus (Ohio) Zoo. The mother of the cubs had never had a litter and didn't seem able to care for her babies. Many young mother cats have trouble raising their first young.

Zookeepers watched the babies closely for two days. By then, the cubs had not nursed, so they were taken to the zoo nursery to be raised by human beings.

Cathryn Hilker, an animal trainer at the Cincinnati Zoo, heard about the cubs. She asked if she could have one to train and use to teach young people about wild animals. Cathryn was offered one of the two cheetah cubs. When the cubs were 10 weeks old, Cathryn visited the Columbus Zoo nursery, sitting on the floor with the cubs playing around her. Even at 10 weeks old the cubs could run very fast. They ran and played, chasing each other, hitting one another lightly with their front paws when the chase ended. After a short rest, the chase began again. This is how young cheetahs play in the wild.

Finally, the smaller cheetah stopped and stood quietly at Cathryn's side. Cathryn had not touched either animal. She wanted the cats to come to her. Standing next to Cathryn and purring loudly—sounding like a huge house cat—the cheetah licked Cathryn's hand with her rough tongue. It felt like wet, scratchy sandpaper against Cathryn's skin.

Cathryn made up her mind. This was definitely the cat she wanted. So the young cheetah, named Maliki, moved from the Columbus Zoo to Cincinnati. She would spend the first year of her life living with Cathryn and her family on a farm near the zoo.

Maliki is a Swahili word from the language spoken in East Africa where cheetahs live in the wild. Cathryn translated the name Maliki into English, and the young cheetah became known as "Angel."

⸺⸙⸺ Angel Grows Up On A Farm ⸺⸙⸺

Angel was about the size of a house cat. Her light tawny coat was covered with black spots and a row of long white hairs stood up along her back from neck to tail. She would lose this stripe by six months of age, but as a small cub, she looked a little like a pincushion.

When she first arrived in a crate at Cathryn's house, Angel stepped out and came face to face with a giant dog, a Great Dane. Dominic was a friendly animal, an experienced substitute parent. During the next week he lay down on the floor and allowed the shy little cheetah to explore every inch of his body. In time, Angel and the dog became playmates.

Like most baby animals, Angel looked for something warm to curl up next to when it was bedtime. Angel chose to sleep near her human friends, usually climbing into the bed with her keeper Cathryn and Cathryn's husband, Hege.

Cathryn spent many hours every day with Angel, who always stayed where Cathryn could see her. This is what baby animals do in the wild. They never stray far from their mothers. Angel had free run of a large, fenced yard where no neighbors could see her.

🐾 Cathryn, Angel, and Carrie Cougar in Mason, Ohio

Angel learned to recognize her trainer's voice and quickly came when she was called. It is important that an animal's trainer be the person who gives it food, since food is part of the reason an animal comes when it is called. Cathryn was always the person to feed Angel.

Imprinting is a key concept in defining the relationship between a human and a wild animal. This means that a young animal learns to look on her keeper as the alpha, the dominant leader. This relationship is very important. Because of it, the animal is obedient to the trainer, as it would be obedient to the most powerful, or dominant, member of its species if it were living in the wild.

Cheetahs must learn to be expert hunters by the time they are two years old. They leave their mothers then and must be able to survive on their own. They cannot be house pets! Angel is a trained animal, but she is also a *wild* animal. She has learned to do what her trainers ask her to do. Wild animals are very different from domestic animals. Dogs and cats have lived with human beings for thousands of years. They have been selectively bred to be gentle and loving to people. Angel will always be a wild animal, but she is so intelligent and well-trained that she can be used as a teacher so that people who see her will understand cheetahs a little better.

By the time Angel was one and a half years old, she weighed 80 pounds, stood 28 inches tall, and measured five and a half feet long from her nose to the tip of her tail. She was nearly full grown and had become an elegant animal.

One day, Cathryn brought home a young mountain lion (cougar) named Carrie. Angel and Dominic had become good friends and Angel looked upon this new arrival as an intruder. Carrie Cougar was smaller and more flexible than Angel. She was able to crawl under the fence and get outside the yard. With a fence to protect her from Angel's fast striking paws, Carrie could play a chasing game with Angel. Up and down the fence they ran until both were tired. A friendship ultimately developed between the two animals which lasted their entire lives.

— ∞ Angel Begins Her Work ∞ —

When Angel was four months old, she and Cathryn started visiting schools. They went to a dozen major cities across the country. Zoos and the media wanted to see her. Angel became the wildlife ambassador of goodwill

🐾 Angel goes to school (1986)

🐾 Top: *Good Morning America* with Host David Hartman; Below: Guest Jimmy Stewart on Regis Philbin's *The Morning Show*

for the Cincinnati Zoo. When the United States sends an ambassador to another country, that person speaks for all of us. Angel's job was to give American children a chance to see a wild animal from another part of the world, and to learn how important cheetahs and other animals are. She and her trainer visited hundreds of schools in the Cincinnati area. More than one million people had the opportunity to meet Angel in person during her eleven-year life span.

Besides visiting schools, Angel appeared on television. Stepping into the spotlight never seemed to trouble Angel (even though her trainer was nervous!). *The Bob Braun Show*, a Cincinnati interview program, was her television debut. Angel was most interested in the thick, round television cables that lay all over the floor. Whenever a camera person moved, Angel tried to grab the cable. Cathryn kept saying "leave it," which is a universal command that all trained animals must learn.

Angel was a guest on many programs. She licked David Letterman's hand. She met Bryant Gumbel of the *Today* show. She appeared on *Good Morning America*, on CNN, and even jumped on the couch with Jimmy Stewart on Regis Philbin's new morning talk show in 1983.[85]

—❦ *Angel Travels Abroad* ❦—

As the wildlife ambassador for the Cincinnati Zoo, Angel took a trip to Central America to the country of Belize. She was the first cheetah ever to visit Belize, as cheetahs are not native to that country.

🐾 The prime minister of Belize and his children meet Angel.

🐾 Top: In the parade through Belize City, an American woman, Sharon Matola, rode on the truck with Angel and Cathryn. Sharon lives in Belize and has started a zoo so that Belizian children can see and learn about their country's native animals. Below: These Belizian children are getting a close look at an endangered cat from another part of the world.

The jaguars of Belize (and throughout Central America) are an endangered species. Angel traveled to Belize (in November 1987) to call attention to the plight of the jaguar. The prime minister of Belize, Manuel Esquivel,

Answering the Call of the Wild
The Remarkable Life of Cathryn Hosea Hilker

hosted a public ceremony to welcome her. Local newspaper reporters and television crews recorded the scene of Angel climbing a long flight of stairs to a platform stage to greet Prime Minister Esquivel and his family.

After the ceremony, Angel rode on a flatbed truck that led a parade through the streets of Belize City. People cheered as Angel sat calmly and stared at the crowds. The final event was a visit to a village school where all the children had written papers about why wild animals are important to their country. The children knew cheetahs were from Africa and could run like the wind.

Cathryn's story about Sharon Matola, founder of the Belize Zoo and Tropical Education Center

Even though the jaguar is native to Belize, Sharon Matola needed a trained and controllable cat like Angel to greet the public. She thought that from a distance people might not notice the differences in appearance between a jaguar and a cheetah. I just got Angel into her crate and on a plane to Miami. At that point, the airport personnel threatened to confiscate Angel. Well even in my mid-fifties I was still six-foot-two and very agile. To their horror, I jumped over the counter to guard Angel's crate. It didn't take long for them to agree to get Angel on the plane to Belize just to get rid of me.

When we arrived, Sharon put Angel in the back of her truck and took us to a place to stay near the capitol city of Belmopan that looked like a small house with a couple of bunkbeds. The open windows—no screens—were big enough for Angel to jump out. Sharon offered to build a cage for Angel out of chicken wire, but that would have been a 30-second escape plan. I had to close the windows and Angel and I spent a hot night without fresh air.

The parade planned for the next day was originally going to have Angel riding through the streets of Belmopan in a wagon pulled by a tractor. I was sure that wouldn't work, so instead Angel sat on the back of a flatbed truck. Hundreds of people lined the streets, all wanting to touch Angel. I don't know how Angel put up with that, but she sat quietly by my side.

I didn't know that part of Sharon's plan was to meet the prime minister of Belize, Manuel Esquivel. We drove on that flatbed truck to a Mayan temple, the steps of which are very much like a step ladder. We were expected to climb up to the top of the pyramid because the prime minister and his family were waiting for us there! Everybody was ready, including the photographers. I just looked at her and said 'Angel, please do this for me.' Thankfully she started going up without me. I walked on my hands and knees because I have terrible acrophobia—I'm terrified of high places, and used to throw up flying on small planes with Hege. When we got to the top, Angel jumped up onto a table, and there was the prime minister with all of his children. They were all petting her. Ron Austing, who was there to take photos, was the Cincinnati Zoo's official photographer for many years!

More than 30 years later, in 2012, Sharon Matola gave the Barrows lecture and received the Cincinnati Zoo's Wildlife Conservation Award, thanking Thane Maynard and Cathryn for helping her get the Belize Zoo started in the 1980s.

—∞ Angel and Her Cat Ambassador Friends ∞—

Angel became so popular that one cat could not fill all the requests to the Cincinnati Zoo for a wild cat visitor. Even her friend Carrie Cougar couldn't entirely fill the demand, so the Zoo added several more beautiful cats to the program. The first addition was a serval—a small spotted cat from Africa—named Missy. Then Tundra, a beautiful snow leopard from the Himalaya Mountains of Asia, joined the troupe.

Missy the Serval

The Zoo built a large, special living area for the cats where they could climb trees and run and play. The Animal Recreation Center (ARC) became home to all the cats once they were fully grown. Collectively, they were called the "Cat Ambassadors" and took turns appearing in programs. When schools requested a visit, Cathryn would load them into a van, drive to the school, and present an educational program.

Tundra the Snow Leopard

The goal of the education program is to teach people about endangered animals and what we need to do to protect them. Students learn that the cats need help from human beings to survive, and that zoo scientists set up captive breeding programs hoping that animals will produce new generations of the species that are in danger of dying out. Thanks to zoo research programs, all captive cheetahs have better diets and may live longer lives.

Imprinting with Angel

I hadn't had Angel too long. Though I had her at home, I hadn't used her that much in our shows. Kris Kalnow was with me when this happened. We stopped for lunch, and Angel was in the back of the van in a big crate so she could move around. I opened the door just to be sure she was okay. Angel sprang to her feet. Her eyes were riveted on me; I had startled her. She just stood there staring directly into my eyes. I still remember this: I went down on my knees and said, 'Angel, I will work for you the rest of my life.'

At that moment I realized she had completely imprinted on me. She trusted only me and wouldn't let anybody else (except Kris) work with her. We were tied together, and I owed that loyalty to her. It was very emotional for me. It's almost like your own infant child snuggling close to develop that maternal bond. It was a bit spooky. People may say that cats don't care, but I know that animals—especially dogs—have their hearts broken when people get rid of them.

If a wild animal is not imprinted on you, they are not safe to use in any kind of exhibit or show. If anything frightens them, a wild animal can become instantly dangerous.

The Angel Fund

The Angel Fund was established at the Cincinnati Zoo in 1992, the year that Cathryn's beloved cheetah Angel died. The Fund's mission is to support work in Cincinnati and internationally, primarily in the African range, for conservation of captive and wild cheetahs (and other cats).

Most of the funds distributed from The Angel Fund from 1992–2005 were to support the Cheetah Conservation Fund's (CCF) main program in Namibia. Financial support of CCF in the range of $50–100,000 a year was used for general operating support, printing costs for educational materials, as well as research, conservation, and education programs.

From 2004–2010, The Angel Fund decided to distribute funds to other cheetah conservation organizations in Africa: Cheetah Outreach in South Africa, CCF programs in Kenya and Botswana, the African Conservation Center, the Niassa Lion Project, and the DeWildt Cheetah Research and Breeding Facility in South Africa.[86]

—⋙ "Angels of Music" ⋘—

Broadway stars Brad Little and Barbara McCulloh "discovered" Cathryn Hilker in 1997 and founded a fundraising event called "Angels of Music" to benefit The Angel Fund. At the time, Little was playing the lead role in the touring company of *Phantom of the Opera*. Parlaying the name of Phantom's alter ego—the angel of music—and the Cincinnati Opera's early residency at the Zoo, the stars (who were married at the time) sprinkled glitter on the Zoo's efforts to help preserve the African cheetah.

Little and McCulloh teamed up with Erich Kunzel, then conductor of the Cincinnati Pops, for five special concerts at Cincinnati's Aronoff Theater

🐾 Angels of Music founders (L-R) Brad Little, Cathryn Hilker, Barbara McCulloh, Erich Kunzel, and Van Ackerman at the Aronoff Theater (1997)

Answering the Call of the Wild
The Remarkable Life of Cathryn Hosea Hilker

during 1997-2008. The concerts netted more than $1.5 million for The Angel Fund. With great admiration, Cathryn says that "the Angels of Music fundraiser was chaired by one of the most successful fundraisers in Cincinnati: Trudi Fullen. All the money went directly to Africa conservation projects."

Van Ackerman and Trudi Fullen with Cathryn (2002)

—∞ *A Postscript About Angel* [87] ∞—

In a memo written to all Zoo staff on February 1, 2007, Cathryn explained an important, and perhaps somewhat unusual, situation involving Angel:

>   This morning Mark Fisher and his staff carefully exhumed Angel.
>   Since our new running area will go directly over her grave, we wanted to retrieve some of her bones to rebury in another place.
>   Angel, as the Zoo's first Cheetah Ambassador, worked with her lifelong partner "Cougar," an American mountain lion, for nearly 12 years. Never refusing, never saying "no," Angel willingly did what she was asked. She changed hearts and educated hundreds of thousands of students and Zoo visitors. With Kris Kalnow, now a Zoo board member, our team worked tirelessly to draw people and animals together in a spirit of understanding.
>   That Angel was ultimately successful is evident in the reality of our new running yard. Without her, I know this would not be possible. Thanks to Kris, this area is fully funded, thus closing the circle of giving.
>   Angel's bones, after 14 years in the earth, are extremely fragile and are now at the Natural History Museum to be cleaned and preserved for future use and display. Angel is the first cheetah ever given to our museum. She will continue teaching. We shall continue working. We shall continue to bring visitors into the circle of respect for wild creatures.
>   Thanks to all who helped with this project. Thanks to all who remember and care about this extraordinary animal.

Cathryn and Sarah (2011)

7

Sahara (Sarah), The Fastest Cheetah in the World (2000–2016)

⟨⟩

In 2012, Sarah shattered the world animal speed record for the standing 100-meter dash, making the human record seem stodgy by comparison. —Multi-media

*S*arah had it all. She was beautiful, charismatic, light on her feet, long and lean, an outstanding ambassador for the Cincinnati Zoo. She and Cathryn were twin souls.

Sarah came to the Cincinnati Zoo when she was only six weeks old and was hand raised at Cathryn's new home in Mason. She was one of the first cheetah cubs in Cincinnati to be raised with a puppy companion, an Anatolian shepherd named Alexa ("Lexi"). An innovation developed three decades ago in Namibia, pairing a dog with a young cheetah is a common worldwide practice today.

Cat Trainer Alicia Sampson recalls a favorite story about Sarah and Cathryn from early in her tenure as a staff member for the Cat Ambassador Program.

One afternoon about 14 years ago we were running Sarah. She was always a challenging cheetah to work with, especially after running. Linda Castañeda and I were trying to get the lure away from her, and in the process, she just got more tangled up in the lure line. This caused Sarah to become angrier and more frustrated by the minute. We needed to be able to cut the line off Sarah, using a long stick with a safety knife at the end, to move her safely out of the yard.

Cathryn then approached the situation and began to fix the problem. It was amazing to stand by and watch Cathryn defuse the situation with such grace and ease. She took in all the cues that Sarah gave her and never wavered. The whole process took about 10 minutes, but it was jaw-dropping to see Cathryn interact with Sarah at a whole different level of understanding of cheetahs.

🐾 Sarah and Lexi

Like her predecessor Angel, Sarah was also a traveler. A particular trip to Washington D.C. in 2004 captured Sarah's "big city" personality! She even met with Cincinnati's U.S. Congressmen Rob Portman and Steve Chabot during the visit.

When Sarah was eight years old, she participated in an international land speed competition with another eight-year-old female cheetah named Nkosazana (which means "princess" in the Nguni Bantu tribal language of South Africa). Zaza, as she was called, lived at the South African Cheetah Outreach organization founded by Annie Beckhelling. The plan was to have

🐾 Cathryn and Sarah in Washington D.C. (2004)

Answering the Call of the Wild
The Remarkable Life of Cathryn Hosea Hilker

🐾 Sarah's 2009 World Record. Cincinnati Zoo staff (L-R) Kathy Watkins, Alicia Sampson, Cathryn Hilker, Linda Castañeda, and Eunice Frahm.

Zaza run a 100-meter dash in South Africa, and several weeks later, Sarah would run the same dash at the Kentucky Speedway. The purpose of the competition was to bring awareness to the plight of wild cheetahs at risk of extinction.

Sarah won with a time of 6.13 seconds, breaking the previous record set in 2001 when a male South African cheetah named Nyana set the 100-meter record in 6.19 seconds.[88] This was big national news at the time.

Three years later, in 2012, *National Geographic* photographers came to Cincinnati to film a dash by 11-year-old Sarah and other cheetahs. *NatGeo* editor Chris Johns told the back story in his Editor's Note for the November 2012 issue:

> I first saw the explosion of speed on the Serengeti Plain 24 years ago. With astonishing swiftness, the cheetah closed the gap between predator and prey, then lay beside the struggling Thomson's gazelle with her jaws around his throat. I wanted a slow-motion replay to document that speed.
>
> Thirteen years later I tried for one on a grassy flat in Namibia. Laurie Marker of the Cheetah Conservation Fund had raised a cheetah

she'd named Chewbaaka. To keep him fit, she'd trained him to chase a lure. (We) set up a dozen cameras programmed to fire eight frames a second in sequence. For more than a week Chewbaaka chased the lure. The results were disappointing. The cat did his job, but we didn't have the technology to do ours.

This summer with the help of *National Geographic's* Big Cats Initiative and Darlene and Jeff Anderson (of Cincinnati), we tried again. The Cincinnati Zoo offered its cheetahs, and cheetah guru Cathryn Hilker offered her expertise. A crew of Hollywood's best set up a 400-foot-long track with a remote-control sled to keep pace with each cat. For three days the cheetahs did their job…Finally, the last night, everything clicked.

Cathryn's elaboration on the editor's introduction tells a slightly different story; the *NatGeo* photography team finally listened to her! "Even though I'm not a photographer, I know how fast cheetahs move. The only way to photograph a cheetah is to start in front of it. The photographers were trying to get their shots by pacing along the side of the cheetah run. That was never going to work. It's sort of like that famous Wayne Gretsky saying—to win in hockey you have to skate where the puck is going."

Tommy T clocked in at 7.19 seconds. Sarah smashed her own world record of 6.13 on the first try by running 100 meters at 61 miles per hour

Answering the Call of the Wild
The Remarkable Life of Cathryn Hosea Hilker

in 5.95 seconds. That's nearly four seconds faster than the Jamaican runner Usain Bolt, who was at that time participating in the summer Olympics, and who held a record for the 100-meter dash of 9.58 seconds.[89] One of *National Geographic's* editors described Sarah as a "polka dotted missile."[90] Her amazing feats of speed earned Sarah a page in Wikipedia.

Sarah's amazing speed records tend to overshadow her wonderful role for nearly 15 years as a cat ambassador for the Cincinnati Zoo. Upon Sarah's passing in 2016, the Zoo's lead trainer for the Cat Ambassador Program, Linda Castañeda, said: "She lived a full life and was a phenomenal ambassador for her species. Sarah was the queen bee around here. She had a very expressive face that communicated what she wanted. And we obliged. She was a dynamic individual, and we were privileged to know her and learn from her. We will all miss the princess cat."[91]

Cathryn's Remembrance of Sarah [92]

Sarah came to live on our Mason farm when she was five weeks old. We intended to raise her with an Anatolian shepherd dog so she could have a companion for herself, but also a companion who could help explain the program of wildlife management in Namibia where these dogs are widely used for predator control. Captive cheetahs are often raised with a dog, as they make excellent companions, but not always. As soon as this little cheetah named Sarah saw our little Anatolian puppy, the cat attacked the dog with such a ferocious attitude that I had to separate them. Their relationship became even worse over the next several days, so I sent the puppy back and got a much bigger and older Anatolian dog. This change worked well. Sarah and Lexi were lifelong companions. They did school shows, summer shows, TV appearances and much more until Lexi retired, leaving Sarah to continue alone.

The joy of running is in the heart and the ancient memory of every cheetah. Sarah was no different. At home in her first few weeks we only did short runs in her fenced-in yard, but the day came when I wanted to see how much more Sarah could do. I was there with her when the joy and the play of running suddenly turned serious for her. It was a Reds baseball cap that triggered her natural instinct to run with utter resolution. To chase, to catch, to hold. I could hardly get the cap away from her. Then she knew what running meant to the cheetah. It made her break her own record for speed, when the *National Geographic* filmed her, at age 11, running 61 mph. 100 meters in 5.95 seconds.

She will be remembered by thousands of school children who heard her loud purr or heard her nails clicking on the tabletop where she stayed during a school program. My memories are imprinted in my heart and mind of a tiny brave little cheetah who grew up and turned into the elegant animal that the mature cheetah is. The claw marks from her tiny little claws when she was a cub remain on my bedspread to this day and the hole she chewed through my zoo jacket and the awkward job I did of sewing it up will remain there for the rest of my life.

We will miss Sarah's eyes, fixed on our eyes, always asking, 'What next?' Indeed Sarah, what next? In your giant shadow of grace other cheetahs will follow your lead, our race to educate and tell your story so that your species can always be waiting to answer, 'What next?'

Answering the Call of the Wild
The Remarkable Life of Cathryn Hosea Hilker

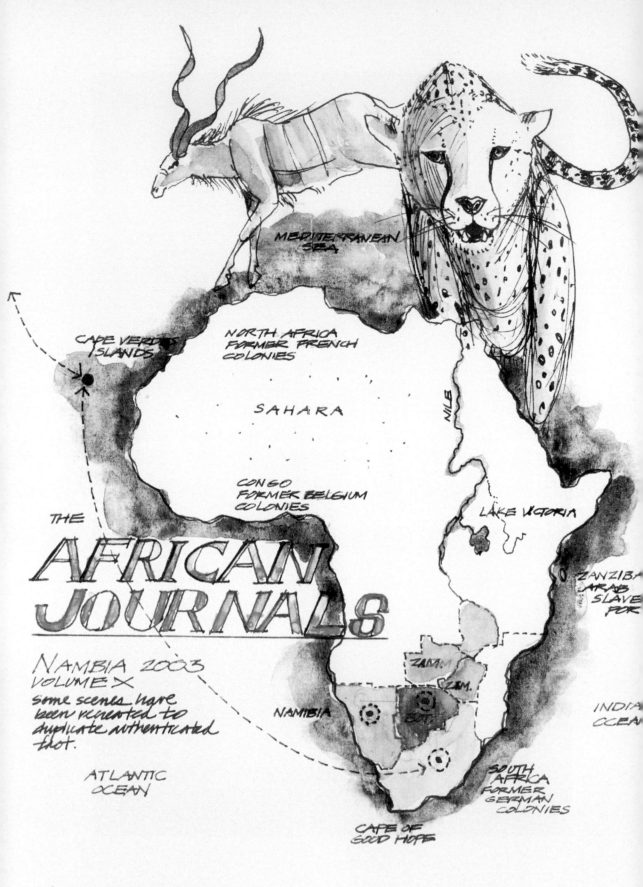

THE
AFRICAN
JOURNALS

MEDITERRANEAN SEA

CAPE VERDE ISLANDS

NORTH AFRICA FORMER FRENCH COLONIES

SAHARA

NILE

CONGO FORMER BELGIUM COLONIES

LAKE VICTORIA

ZANZIBAR ARAB SLAVE POR

NAMBIA 2003
VOLUME X
some scenes have
been recreated to
duplicate authenticated
fact.

ZAM

ZAM.
BOT.

NAMIBIA

INDIA OCEAN

ATLANTIC OCEAN

SOUTH AFRICA FORMER GERMAN COLONIES

CAPE OF GOOD HOPE

Drawing by Gary Hang Lee (2003)

ANTARCTIC

8

The African Journals

My Mom was very much a farm girl from Mason, Ohio. Those were her roots, her anchor, even as she grew internationally to support wildlife. In her heart, she loves Ohio more than any place else on earth. I think her work reflects that. —Carl Hilker III

The Cincinnati Zoo's practice of hosting global expeditions started in 1964 when then-director Bill Hoff and his wife, Lynn, spent two weeks in Central East Africa viewing and photographing big game. In future years, regular "safari" trips for Zoo patrons included trips to the Galapagos Islands, Central America, and the Antarctic. These trips formed the foundation of the Zoo's emerging laser focus on education and awareness of the habitats, circumstances, and future prospects of wildlife animals.

Cathryn's passion for Africa was cemented during her 1957 trip with the Zoo's part-time veterinarian, Dr. Byron Bernard. Though more than 25 years would elapse before she returned to Africa in 1984, Cathryn made up for lost time during the next quarter century, taking many trips culminating in a celebration of her 80th birthday in 2011. Most of her safaris were educational journeys sponsored by the Cincinnati Zoo—some co-sponsored with the Cheetah Conservation Fund—for small groups of avid Zoo supporters. One group of nine Cincinnati women dubbed their great adventure in 2007 "The African Queens."

Cathryn curated trips to Africa for many special people in her life, including a 2006 trip to Kenya co-sponsored with Cincinnati Pops Maestro Erich Kunzel. He was a big fan of the Cincinnati Zoo and regularly invited Cathryn on stage during Pops performances at Riverbend.

🐾 Top: "The African Queens" in Namibia (2007); Below: Cathryn with Brad Little

Broadway stars Brad Little and Barbara McCulloh fell in love with Cathryn and her cheetahs when the couple first met her in 1996. McCulloh was in Cincinnati during a break between leading roles in New York. Her then-husband, Brad Little, was on national tour playing the title role in *Phantom of the Opera*.

Coincidentally, McCulloh attended the Christmas Hunt at the Camargo Hunt Club. At the evening reception, McCulloh was enchanted by watching

Answering the Call of the Wild
The Remarkable Life of Cathryn Hosea Hilker

Cathryn work the room while extolling the virtues of Africa and her farm. In her inimitable way, Cathryn approached this stranger at the event and said bluntly, "Who are you?" When McCulloh responded that she was playing the role of Anna in *The King and I* on Broadway, Cathryn promptly began to sing one of the show's centerpiece songs.

Their friendship was instantly cemented: "Cathryn is unforgettable to most who meet her. She's an extraordinary woman in what she has endeavored to do and accomplish." McCulloh even joined Cathryn at her farm to help quarantine with Moya, the cheetah gifted to Cincinnati by South African Cheetah Outreach.

🐾 Erich Kunzel, Kenya trip co-sponsor

A trip to Africa with the Hilkers was inevitable. In 2000, Barbara and Brad were treated to a private tour of Namibia. "We traveled in a four-person plane with Hege as our pilot. Hege liked to push Cathryn to the limit of her patience. One time, flying into the sunset in a small plane with few controls to navigate in the dark, we ran out of gas. We eventually landed in a field and found a place to stay."

Four of Cathryn's many trips to Africa were documented in her own journals and in stories written or shared by others during interviews. These four stories offer intimate perspectives revealing the many ways and reasons that Cathryn fell in love with Africa, homeland of her beloved cheetahs.

1988 | by Cathryn Hilker

In September 1988, Zoo ambassador Cathryn hosted a group of nine Cincinnatians on a tour of South Africa and Botswana. She chronicled this trip by hand in an ordinary steno pad–a symbol of her thrifty nature–which was rescued from the bottom of her old USO trunk filled to the brim with 65 years of memorabilia! In her own words:

While part of the group slept in to recover from our long flight to Johannesburg, South Africa, a few of us went to the DeWildt Cheetah Breeding Center. Ann van Dyk is a grand woman who took us all over her station. They have over 100 cheetahs; we saw 40-50 and lots of babies. We saw the King Cheetah they are sending to our Zoo in exchange for a white tiger. Her animals are her life. She is as dedicated to cheetahs as I am.

We flew three and a half hours over the Okavango Delta in Botswana to Mambo Camp run by Karen Ross and her husband. Ross wrote *Jewel of the Kalahari Okavango* which was published last year. After a game safari drive and dinner that night, a hyena walked right by our campfire. We could see his eyes shine in the dark.

It was cold when we were awakened at 6:30 a.m. for our morning drive. Our guide was good at spotting game, whereas I saw only humps of dirt. We saw a good-looking male lion who allowed us to get fairly close before threatening to charge the vehicle. At first I could not see the Southern Cross constellation, but what a thrill when I finally did! All is so quiet and perfect. Indeed, man seems to be the interloper.

Karen told us a neat story. The local tribe calls the Milky Way 'the backbone of the earth.' I grew up looking at it in the darkness of our farm. I doubt my son Carl has even seen it. Air pollution has blocked it from our vision. What a comment on our values.

We left Mambo Camp for an all-day trip to Lechwee Island. We had to cross deep swamp water to get to the boat to cross the lagoon. Our 'swamp buggy' broke down during the crossing. Two of the men were covered with grease after fixing the buggy with a cotter pin, but that fix only lasted about 100 yards. We had to walk through the swamp the rest of the way. I got a few good 'blackmail' pictures from that adventure.[93]

We had a wonderful day, but it still doesn't seem like Africa to me. My emotional Africa is the vast plains, mountains, and massive ancient herds of East Africa. Botswana is great, and the native folks have treated us so well, but I feel a little strange here. East Africa may well be 'home.'

Then we were off to the Machaba Camp. Botswana has more than 50,000 elephants. We went on a sensational evening game run and saw great herds of elephants. During our morning game run we saw evidence of enormous elephant damage. Our guide said the land can sustain the damage, but something tells me it is close to a problem. It is the end of the dry season, and heavy mid-October rains are on the way from Angola. The trees need this reprieve from the elephants eating the leaves and breaking small branches.

I learned a new phrase while we were waiting for our delayed plane to take us on to Shinde Camp in the Okavango Delta: TAB. It stands for 'that's Africa baby.'

When we arrived at the camp, our host told us during lunch about how the government is spraying for the Tsetse fly. The fish and birds are dying, and he feels this is the first step to opening up the Delta to cattle. They will bring an end to yet another beautifully balanced ecosystem in Africa. Hopefully Botswanan folks can learn from the mistakes of others and use their beautiful lands not only to truly benefit their people but also to preserve one of the world's great nature treasures.

We went fishing on a mokoro,[94] poking through the swamps as our guide's ancestors did a hundred years ago. Several guests caught bream, which we cooked and had before a dinner of Botswanan beef. The next day we went on a walking safari, passing old bulls along the way. Our guide carried a gun, which I thought was wrong—we could have passed them at a safer distance and not needed the gun.

On our departure flight to Kubu Island, we flew low at 250 feet over the Kalahari Desert. We were able to see how the Delta changes to arid land and then turns into the salt pans of the Makadikadi Basin, the remains of a lake that once covered the desert. We flew over several cordon fences that stretch endlessly across the land. Those are the fences that kept the migratory wildebeest from water and caused the death of 50,000 animals. This travesty was another missing link in our fragile chain of life.

As we were leaving Kubu Island by helicopter, we saw fresh elephant tracks leading out across the salt pan. What are they doing way out here? It was almost like Hemingway's leopard: 'What was he searching for at this altitude?' There was no answer to this question....

Our flight to Victoria Falls in Zambia took us over the Zambezi River. Our hotel was right out of central casting in the days of British control when the country was known as Rhodesia. My first view of the Falls took me back to all of my childhood fantasies about them—tales of English explorers and what those early experiences were like.

The Hilkers' month-long trip to Africa in May 2003 was co-sponsored by the Cincinnati Zoo and the Cheetah Conservation Fund (CCF). The first two weeks of the trip included a city visit to Cape Town, South Africa; a tour of the CCF ranch near Windhoek, Namibia; a safari experience at the Desert Rhino Camp in Palmwag, Namibia; and a pilgrimage to Victoria Falls in Zambia.

In mid-May, Cathryn and Hege connected with a larger group of people from Cincinnati for a grand tour of Namibia. The purpose of the tour was in part to show the results of contributions from The Angel Fund to CCF in support of cheetah conservation.

One of the guests (front row, second from left) was architect/landscape architect Gary Hang Lee of the Philadelphia-based firm CLR Design. Specializing in zoo design based on habitat immersion—transforming visitor experiences and maximizing humane treatment of wild animals—the firm had been hired by then-director Gregg Hudson (back row, right) to accelerate implementation of the Zoo's master plan.

A witty storyteller and accomplished artist, Lee chronicled the Namibian adventure in words, drawings, and photos, all presented in a journal as a

Guests of Cincinnati Zoo and Cheetah Conservation Fund

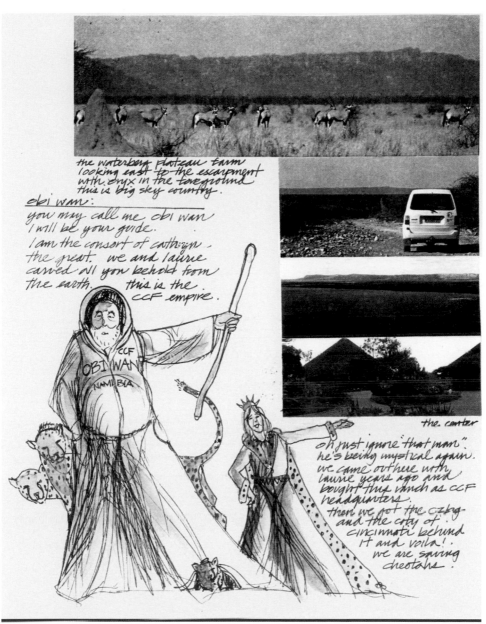

the waterberg plateau farm
looking east to the escarpment
with oryx in the foreground
this is big sky country.

obi wan:
you may call me obi wan
i will be your guide.
i am the consort of cathryn.
the great. we and laurie
carved all you behold from
the earth.   this is the
                  CCF empire.

CCF
OBI WAN
NAMIBIA

the center

oh just ignore "that man".
he's being mystical again.
we came out here with
laurie years ago and
bought this ranch as ccf
headquarters.
then we got the czkg.
and the city of .
cincinnati behind
it and voila!
we are saving
cheetahs.

🐾 "Obi-Wan" Hege

souvenir for participants. He gave nicknames to group leaders Cathryn ("Empress Dowager") and Hege ("Obi-Wan").

The CCF farm is located right next to the magnificent Waterberg Plateau, an escarpment along the northern boundary of the farm. The plateau itself is now a game reserve.

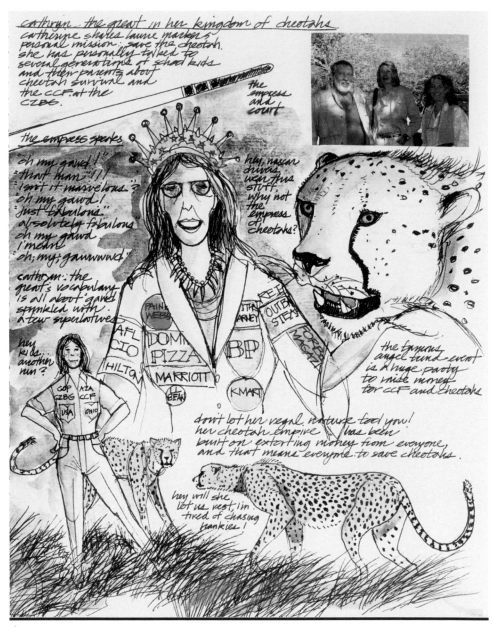

🐾 "Empress Dowager" Cathryn

Hege's description of the area brings the Waterberg Plateau to life, as does Gary Lee's photo. "This land is magical. The sky and plateau light up at sunset, my favorite time to fly and to buzz the kudu and red hartebeest herds. There are rhino and leopard in the escarpment reserve. Lots of small antelope and birds. A real Eden."

Waterberg Plateau

Gary Lee had a few cheeky things to say about Hege's sunset strolls through the sky. "Hege is a pretty good pilot, but he does scare the shit out of every warthog or antelope within fifty miles. He is also wing commander for the CCF and regularly patrols the Waterberg Plateau. Hege is a buzzer. He likes to aim the airplane at something and buzz it. You name it, he'll buzz it. The animals say, 'Oh God, it's Hege again. That man needs a real job!!'"

In Lee's story, he says that "Carl and Cathryn bought the original farmstead and the CCF has since added adjacent parcels. The farms here are big. They all average about 10,000 acres which provides just enough water to support 1,000 cattle. CCF now has over 100,000 acres." By 2003, the plans for a new CCF complex had evolved to include an education center, library, offices, service center, veterinary hospital and research center, and a stable for goats and horses. Lee described the environment where CCF does its work:

"Namibia is just like Texas—big sky, big country, lots of fences. Cheetahs have to deal with cattle fences which bisect the grasslands (to make hunting for game tough, which is good). A typical cheetah territory overlaps several ranches, so cheetahs have to cross many fences to get supper. The area is also shifting to thickets of impenetrable scrub—like mesquite in Texas—and cheetahs can't hunt in this dense jungle. Clearing strategies are important."

Before Cathryn Hilker was Cathryn Hilker, she was Cathryn Hosea. She grew up on a farm surrounded by animals, surrounded by growing things. She became an accomplished horsewoman, riding beautiful, big horses over steep jumps and deep motes, chasing the sounds of hounds in full cry. Animals spoke to her. She heard them.

She also loved Shakespeare. He spoke to her too. She and her life-long friend, Joan Rollman Musenkamp, would challenge each other to memorize Shakespeare's lines, sonnets, soliloquies, and speeches, trying to "best" each other by reciting, from memory, without stumbling or forgetting. The one who made it all the way through won. Cathryn Hosea was as good at that as she was at riding horses.

Fast forward to Thursday, April 29, 2004, in the High Desert of Namibia. Now Cathryn Hilker, her ties to Africa drew her there many times, to many countries, till she owned a part of one, and the cheetahs owned a greater part of her. Her beloved cheetahs took her there; and they and their native places never left her.

On this particular trip, a mythic guide appeared at the edge of a Namibian dirt airstrip, in a pared-down safari vehicle, to meet Cathryn and her group: Chris Bakkes. He would show her his place under that huge Namibian desert sky and regale her and her group with stories. Chris—red-haired, red-bearded, deep voiced, laughing eyes, strikingly strong presence, filled with stories—was indeed a match for Cathryn Hilker and her boisterous self. Oh, and he had only one whole arm and a half of another. It seems he had a fight with a crocodile. He lost his forearm in that battle. However, he was not "bested" by that croc.

Cathryn with Chris Bakkes

During that safari, there was a night in that high desert place, dinner in a canvas tent, a fire crackling outside of it. After dinner, chairs were arranged around that beckoning fire, Scotch shimmering burnt orange in glasses. Then, there was a moment when someone mentioned Shakespeare. It had to have been Chris, who looked like he had just walked out of one of Will's plays. All he needed was a broad sword.

The "St. Crispin's Day Speech" from *Henry V | Act IV | Scene 3 | 18-67* was mentioned. That's all that was needed, just the mentioning.

Cathryn stood up from her chair. Chris stood up from his. They faced each other, eye to eye. Nodded at each other, as opponents in a tournament will do. And they began in unison.

"The fewer men, the greater share of honour."

All gathered around the radiant fire that night fell silent. Two voices rose as they recited, from memory, those legendary lines. The words rose up into that night sky like sparks from the fire.

Until there was a moment, a pause, a loud intake of breath and Chris just stopped. He nearly howled. He could not remember the rest. He lost his place. The words left him, standing there.

Cathryn, not missing one iambic pentameter beat, kept going, her voice growing louder with each line. Every word that Will had penned she hurled at that one-armed chieftain until he collapsed in his chair and sat there, listening.

"Old men forget; yet all shall be forgot,"

Cathryn continued as if she were King Henry himself, outlasting this man who, surely, was not used to that! She finished that mythic speech, alone, eyes shining, voice strong, arms raised to the African sky.

"We few, we happy few, we band of brothers;"

Chris sat there dumbstruck. Chris was being outdone by an older woman from Mason, Ohio, in the United States, who loved animals and Shakespeare and had followed her passion for and her work with African cheetahs to a high-desert place called Palamvag.

Cathryn Hosea Hilker "bested" Chris Bakkes in front of a fire, under a midnight blue sky thick with stars shining above that moment in time, by as ancient a fire as there can be.

When she finished with the last line, hand above her head...

"That fought with us upon Saint Crispin's day."

...the applause and the laughter resounded out through the night. And then, the defeated chieftain was the first to rise from his seat, raise his glass of Scotch, and pay homage to the unequivocal champion of that storied evening; his, the loudest laugh of all.

Ever after, if I close my eyes, I can see that fire and lean back in my chair; and there I see these two captivating characters standing, one arm's length apart. And "the challenge" begins...again.

Shakespeare's King Henry V Speech in Act IV

This day is call'd the feast of Crispian.

He that outlives this day, and comes safe home,

Will stand a tip-toe when this day is nam'd,

And rouse him at the name of Crispian.

He that shall live this day, and see old age,

Will yearly on the vigil feast his neighbours,

And say "To-morrow is Saint Crispian."

Then will he strip his sleeve and show his scars,

And say "These wounds I had on Crispin's day."

Old men forget; yet all shall be forgot,

But he'll remember, with advantages,

What feats he did that day. Then shall our names,

Familiar in his mouth as household words—

Harry the King, Bedford and Exeter,

Warwick and Talbot, Salisbury and Gloucester—

Be in their flowing cups freshly remember'd.

This story shall the good man teach his son;

And Crispin Crispian shall ne'er go by,

From this day to the ending of the world,

But we in it shall be remember'd—

We few, we happy few, we band of brothers;

For he to-day that sheds his blood with me

Shall be my brother; be he ne'er so vile,

This day shall gentle his condition;

And gentlemen in England now a-bed

Shall think themselves accurs'd they were not here,

And hold their manhoods cheap whiles any speaks

That fought with us upon Saint Crispin's day.

🐾 Lily Maynard (left) and Cathryn Hilker (second from right) meet African Hosts

—∞∞ 2011 | Lily Maynard [95] ∞∞—

Lily Maynard, daughter of Thane and Kathleen Maynard, accompanied Cathryn to Africa in 2011 to celebrate Cathryn's 80th birthday. Just the two of them! She and Cathryn had been close friends since Lily was a young child. Lily had just graduated from Smith College where she had done her undergraduate honors thesis on cheetah behavior, and she was ready for an adventure before settling into her post-college pursuits.

Cathryn said that she wanted to visit every site in Africa where The Angel Fund supported cheetah conservation. That was thrilling, but so daunting! We literally had to get out a map of Africa to realize that we couldn't possibly go everywhere because of how far The Angel Fund had reached with funding. It would have been a very long trip. We had to decide: Eastern or Southern Africa? Cathryn chose Eastern Africa, her favorite part of the continent.

I felt lucky to be her companion and assistant throughout the trip to help her assess future grants from The Angel Fund. She was

🐾 African Cows Courtesy of SORALO

a bit unsteady on her feet, so I was also her guide. We went to two sites in Kenya. First was the South Rift Association of Land Owners (SORALO), a project supported by The Angel Fund. SORALO works in many communities in the valley between Amboseli National Park and the Maasai Mara Game Reserve where the pastoral Maasai people make daily choices to co-exist with carnivores. We stayed at a tented camp in the beautiful dry savanna, learning from people whose culture is based on conservation. Herds of cattle, goats, and sheep live alongside lion prides, spotted and striped hyenas, and many small carnivores.

But our Maasai hosts knew Cathryn most wanted to see a cheetah.

I joined the researchers and game scouts on their pre-dawn drive searching for cheetah tracks in the Maasai group's wide-ranging territory. As the sun rose, we found two male cheetahs basking in the golden morning light and radioed back to camp with instructions to bring Cathryn to our location. I was amazed that they found us after we had driven in circles and twists for hours!

Answering the Call of the Wild
The Remarkable Life of Cathryn Hosea Hilker

After watching the cheetahs, SORALO director John Kamanga took us to visit his herd of cows. Cathryn exclaimed with joy. While the SORALO team had worked hard before dawn to make sure Cathryn could see cheetahs, in the end the farm girl from Ohio was more excited to see cattle and talk to other farmers.

Then we visited Actions for Cheetah in Kenya (ACK). It was a hard trip. Kenya wasn't an easy place to navigate because there were no planes flying to these remote sites. We bounced our way down some very rough roads in a jeep. Cathryn's back was bad, so she had to wear a large brace and sit on some pillows to protect her from the hard bounces. She was intrepid, though, so we just kept going.

I vividly remember stumbling into the large canvas tent that Cathryn and I were going to share at the ACK site. Cathryn had a little tantrum because she was tired and aching and didn't want to stay, but we had just spent seven hours driving there and it wasn't really possible to turn around. I gave her a piece of chocolate, encouraged

🐾 Dr. Amy Dickman (front, center) in Ruaha

Mark Portman, Lily Maynard, Cathryn Hilker, and Colleen and Keith Begg's family

her to sit down on her cot, and promised we would be all right. That seemed to cheer her up.

A few days later we went to Tanzania and got on a little plane to visit Amy Dickman, the founder of the Ruaha Carnivore Project. Amy and her team are amazing researchers who study the wild landscape of Ruaha National Park far from bustling parks full of tourists such as Serengeti. We camped at Ruaha as well, and got to meet local people for whom Amy and her team provide health and educational incentives to promote conservation. This was very inspiring to me. Researchers like Amy eventually led me where I am now: completing a doctorate and becoming Conservation Program Manager for Disney's Animal, Science, and Environment Program.

But we didn't stop there. We went to one more site supported by The Angel Fund: the Niassa Lion Project. Ruaha is not a national park, but rather a big area of preserved land in northern Mozambique with huge mountainous rocks. We were joined for this part of the trip by Mark Portman, a Cincinnatian who was working in Tanzania at the time on his way to becoming an expert in fisheries conservation. Our hosts were Niassa's researchers Colleen and Keith Begg.

Our itinerary instructions were quite interesting. Get on a big plane, then a smaller plane. From the coastal city of Pemba, Mozambique, go to a bigger town—really a tribal village in the Niassa Game Reserve. Land on an airstrip along the river. Get into the awaiting Land Rover. Drive for four hours. Get in a canoe with your suitcases and paddle downstream until you find the research camp.

We did all of that. I sat in the front of the canoe, Cathryn sat in the middle, and our guide was in the back of the canoe paddling past hippos and giant crocodiles.

After a long while, we eventually made it to the camp at a very rural site. When we arrived, our hosts said, 'Oh, we're so glad you made it! Last week one of the crocodiles bit a canoe in half.' They later told us that they sleep in a treehouse for safety. We were glad we made it as well.

Cathryn and Angel (1987)

9

Leaving a Legacy: A Portrait of Cathryn Hosea Hilker

Teacher • Naturalist • Writer • Storyteller • Cat Trainer
Conservationist • Problem Solver

Her lifetime conservation work has made her uniquely synonymous with the principal object of that work—Hilker and cheetahs just go together. She has been called "a cheetah in a woman's body;" her understanding of cheetahs is intuitive.[96]

By now it should be abundantly clear why Cathryn Hosea Hilker would be honored for her work in cheetah conservation by her Cincinnati community and by every important person and institution that has defined a segment of her life. What may not be a readily apparent is how deeply so many people *feel* about Cathryn in a unanimous chorus of love and admiration.

Cathryn imagined that her biography could be told entirely through the lens of her cats. But, of course, that would miss so many nuances and accomplishments of this remarkable woman.

If there is one word that rises above all others to describe her, it is passion. Determined is not far behind. She's a woman who never took no for an answer.

The Essence of Cathryn Hosea Hilker

When asked what Carl III admires most about his mom, he said, "One of the things my mom taught me was to do something you're passionate about. Find your passion and follow it. That's clearly what she did. She was very much a role model in that regard. Something I really admire about her is that she was always willing to share her passion with people.

Some of her greatest relationships to further conservation came about because of that spirit. There were so many times where she would just randomly meet people who would express interest, and it would just open incredible doors for her. My mom has done a great deal internationally to raise awareness about cheetahs and their preservation. She made a good name for herself around the world as one of only a handful of people who could train and work with cheetahs and other large cats and use them in education work.

But in some ways her spirit is anchored more in Ohio than it is in Africa. For Cincinnati, I think that is probably her strongest legacy. She really loves where she is from and did a lot of good work for the city and state as well as the world. She worked on international efforts, but it was about Ohio for my mom."

She is tall, leggy, attractive, graceful, elegant, poised, focused, and fast, just like her beloved cheetahs. A 1997 feature article in the *Deseret News* (Salt Lake City, Utah) led with the notion that one couldn't help but notice the similarities between Cathryn and her then-partner cheetah Maya. "The woman and the cheetah share an innate grace and beauty. They are so comfortable within their angular, raw-boned bodies that their movements appear as effortless as breathing. Their trust, too, is complete. It is no wonder that the cheetah has so deeply touched Cathryn Hilker."[97]

Cathryn's son Carl says that she inherited these qualities from her father, the man she most admires. "Even though she was a nerdy type, she really did make an effort to look good, and she was very graceful. She got that from my grandfather who was a very elegant man well into his nineties—very straight, very poised, a quiet yet strong presence. She continues to be that way now." Even as she approaches her 90th birthday, Cathryn remains every bit of six feet tall, walking and sitting with such erect posture as can only come from years of perfecting horsemanship (and perhaps therapeutic recovery from a few back injuries).

Cathryn is strong and independent. It would have been easier for her to follow a path that others had already created or walked before. But she made a path for herself.

She is extremely well read, able to quote Shakespeare and poetry off the top of her head. And she is guaranteed to say whatever she thinks. (According to one person interviewed for this book, "You don't want to put a hot mic on her.")

She is genuine and magnetic, full of charisma. People don't love her a little; they love her a lot!

Her friend for 60 years, Cathy Jacob, puts a fine note on this perspective. "How do I put into words what a lifetime of friendship means? You're a horse-woman, musician, singer, educator, wildlife expert with cheetahs, a kind soul, and my friend for our lifetimes. We have hunted, traveled, enjoyed the zoo and their beautiful cats, enjoyed the beautifully simple things of nature, musicals, each other's deep and warm friendship. You are my big sister who shared and taught me many things that I will never forget. There is no way to fully describe my love for you."

Another dear friend, Cora Ogle, befriended Cathryn twenty years ago on a life adventure quite different from others whose connection to Cathryn

🐾 Diane Babcock, Kris Kalnow, Cora Ogle, and Cathryn Hilker

is through cheetahs or horses. Although Cora is a big Cincinnati Zoo fan and knew Cathryn from that context as well as the Camargo Hunt, it wasn't until they were both on a plane to Florida that their friendship took flight. Cora and her husband Jim were headed south for a visit to their home on North Captiva Island. Cathryn was traveling solo on a nostalgia trip to visit some of the places in Florida where she had spent time growing up.

Always quick with an invitation, Cora asked Cathryn to visit North Captiva. Several days later, Cathryn arrived and stayed for a week! Cathryn and Cora bonded over their shared spirit of adventure, both recalling with glee a momentous walk when they happened upon a nude beach. Cathryn was surprised but nonplussed. (Cora already knew about it.)

Back home in Cincinnati, they shared a love of music. Cora was on the Cincinnati Symphony Orchestra board at the time, and when they attended concerts Cathryn knew all the music. Cora was surprised to learn that Cathryn was an accomplished pianist in addition to her ability to quote reams of Shakespeare. "She's really a renaissance woman. People think of her as a farm girl—as does Cathryn herself—and as a cheetah lady, but she is so much more than that."

Cathryn is a natural leader. She always had an intuitive understanding that, even as just one person, there was something quite meaningful she could do to save her beloved cheetahs. Her friend Diane Babcock describes this special quality perfectly: "She infected us with her joyous love of cats and shared them with so many people—from school children to seniors—enabling all of us to have first-hand experiences with them and to share her wonder of cats. Like a pied piper, she led us in the preservation of the cheetah."

Cathryn is a humble woman. Craig Maier, former CEO of Frisch's, sums it up this way: "She just steps aside for everyone else to get all the credit for everything. But none of that would happen without her. She is a woman of great modesty about her achievements. If you're not trying to take ownership of success, then success is a lot easier because everybody else feels really good about it. And before you know it, things get done."

Everyone who participated in developing this book offered myriad examples of the things Cathryn led, achieved, and caused to happen by sheer dint of her passion and will. Stubborn? Maybe. Just do it! In Cathryn's world, that's how she sees it.

Most people describe Cathryn as a charmer—certainly not naïve, but definitely possessing a degree of guilelessness in the immediate and profound effect she has upon meeting people from all walks of life. Call it love at first sight. Thane Maynard shared that Cathryn could always walk into a room and attract a flock of people who would become instant admirers.

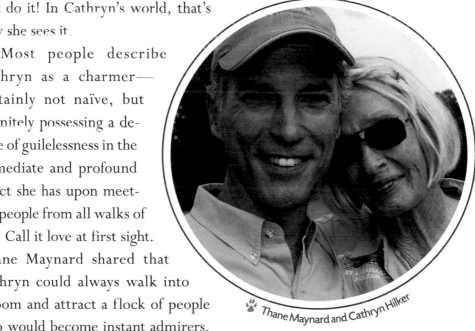

Thane Maynard and Cathryn Hilker

Cathryn would probably say it was because she was so tall. Thane would rebut that notion by underscoring the warm and engaging way that Cathryn relates to all people regardless of their position or stature—physical or otherwise.

Christina Anderson

Several of Cathryn's colleagues at the Cincinnati Zoo shared their great respect for Cathryn's commitment to cheetah conservation, her seemingly innate ability to work with cheetahs, and her excellence as a teacher:

Since meeting Cathryn, I have always felt like she is a member of my family. We've shared so much laughter and fun times together. I love the story she told me about looking a cheetah in the eye and knowing that it was her destiny to help protect and save them. She has been a great educator to so many people regarding cheetah conservation. I feel honored to know her and be one of her friends. *Christina Anderson, Executive Assistant to Thane Maynard, Zoo Director*

Cathryn is really a cheetah trapped in a woman's body—that is how she can understand what a cheetah is thinking and know its next move. She can communicate with any cheetah through an unspoken bond they share. I am lucky to have learned from her and spend my career trying to understand the cheetah the way she does. *Linda Castañeda, Lead Cat Trainer*

Cathryn is an amazing trainer. She is truly gifted. I have learned so much from her, and from watching her work, which has been an amazing gift to me. I am so fortunate to have worked with Cathryn, the very best cheetah trainer there is.

—*Alicia Sampson, Cat Trainer*

According to son Carl, his mother is reliably so focused on her passion for cheetahs and her mission at a public event that she isn't easily impressed by stars of any sort. It's genuine, not an affectation, thus endearing her to people who would typically be stalked for an autograph. Several people shared this story about Bill Russell (of basketball's Boston Celtics fame) as their favorite Cathryn anecdote:

Trainers Linda Castañeda and Alicia Sampson with Sarah

National Geographic hosted an event in Washington D.C. at which Cathryn happened to be seated next to basketball great Bill Russell. After exchanging giggles about how tall they both are, and that therefore they must be related, the ensuing pleasantries led to Cathryn's inevitable question when meeting a new person, "And what do you do?" As the story goes, Bill responded that he was on the board of *National Geographic* and that he used to play basketball. Cathryn did not connect those dots, so proceeded to pontificate about never liking the slam-dunk move in basketball. Bill is reported by multiple observers to have replied, "Well, ma'am, I sort of started that trend."

Another fabled story, embedded in the lore of Cathryn, is that when she asked Frisch's Restaurants owner Jack Maier for sponsorship support, he said yes time and time again—just because she asked and because he trusted her implicitly.

And those millions of starstruck children (and their parents) who Cathryn enticed to learn a bit about an endangered species while enchanting them with leaping cheetahs? Gaga.

One of Cathryn's superpowers is her ability to quiet a crowd of noisy kids and take command of a crowded classroom or auditorium. She never had to ask a group of children to quiet down. She would just bring the microphone up to her cheetah's throat so the guttural sound of the cat purring reverberated across the room. Even teenagers would sit still without moving or making another sound. With little kids, she would put dark tear marks on their faces so they could experience how cheetahs deflect bright light.

Thank you, Cathryn!

"We got letters of appreciation after our school visits that would just melt your heart," according to Kris Kalnow, Cathryn's partner in wildlife education for nearly 15 years.

These thank you letters from Cathryn's personal papers, all dated 1985, demonstrate the range of her work in the community and the depth of appreciation for it:

"I was fortunate to have seen one of your 'shows' and wanted to let you know that I fully share your love and concern for wild animals. I wish there were more people like you and Cathy and the rest of the staff at the Cincinnati Zoo (for, if there were, I'm certain that this would be a better world to live in)." *Michael Hoeferlin, Director of Film Productions, United Way of America*

Kris Kalnow and Cathryn Hilker

"U.A.O. (University Activities Organization) would like to thank you for the fabulous program on Wednesday night. Both students and faculty remarked on your extensive knowledge as well as excellent rapport with the cats." *George Anderson, President, U.A.O., University of Dayton*

"Thank you for taking time from your busy schedule to entertain the students at the Robert E. Lucas School with your exciting cat demonstrations. Your activity has become an essential part of our annual overnight campout." *Noel Taylor, Principal, and Kathryn Dickens, Assistant Principal, Princeton School District*

"Fantastic is the first word that comes to mind when I think of your presentation. It was outstanding—by far the best that I heard at the conference. I appreciate your taking the time and trouble to prepare such an excellent paper and also bringing Angel to Columbus. I can tell you, from the comments I heard, that you impressed a lot of people." Gordon Hubbel, *Director of Education/Veterinarian, Miami (Florida) Metro Zoo*

"Thanks so much for sharing your beautiful cats with us. Students and faculty were all very impressed with your exciting, informative program. What a great way to learn." *Gayle Hegwood, Principal, Batesville (Indiana) Community School Corporation*

"I know I speak for hundreds of others when I say 'THANK YOU' for sharing yourself and Angel with all of us at the Minnesota Zoo. Without Angel, the Zoo's advertising agency would have had a hard time producing its commercial spot for our special summer exhibit of cheetahs." *James Rognlie, Deputy Director, Minnesota Zoological Garden*

A selection of the many accolades commemorating Cathryn's 75ᵗʰ birthday in 2006 also helps to paint a portrait of the regard she enjoys from many admirers:

Dr. Betsy Dresser, *Founder of the Center for Research of Endangered Wildlife (CREW), Cincinnati Zoo & Botanical Garden:* "I used to watch you jumping cats from barrel to barrel on an old stage with props that you made. Everyone in the audience would cheer for your cheetahs and whatever else you had jumping, and you would make sure they knew that somewhere in there was a conservation message. I so wanted to be like you one day, contributing to wildlife conservation. It's your incredible passion and sense of humor that makes you so outstanding."

J. Michael Fay, *an American ecologist, conservationist, and wildlife photographer* best known for spending 455 days walking 2,000 miles across Africa's Congo Basin: "When you were born, there were fewer than a billion people on earth, the tropical and boreal forests were still completely intact, and no one could fathom that icecaps would melt and polar bears would be endangered. We still have lots of work to do."

Jack Hanna, *Former Director of the Columbus Zoo and Aquarium* and star of the reality television show *Into the Wild:* "Cathryn was a pioneer in teaching conservation through education with her amazing cheetahs. History will show that Cathryn and the Cincinnati Zoo played a great part in preserving the magnificent cheetah population. Cathryn has always been an innovator, and because of her work, millions of people throughout the world know about the cheetah."

Erich Kunzel, *Former Conductor of the Cincinnati Pops:* "She's totally nuts! It started many years ago when she married another nutcase, Hege. A lot of his zaniness rubbed off on her. Recently she decided to fall off her favorite horse. She gave us some other goddamned excuse, but we know otherwise. So during the magnificent festivities of the 'Angels of Music' concert to raise money for the cheetah fund, she shows up in a wheelchair and wheels herself all over the place. 'Ole Gimpy' then gimps up on stage!"

Barbara McCulloh and Brad Little, *Broadway and musical theater actors:* "From the first moment of meeting the nine-foot-tall woman, through the horses, the hunts, the cheetahs, the concerts, and of course, Africa, you have been a wonderful force and

> impetus in our lives. Whether in the company of hundreds or alone in the sands of Namibia, you've shone a light on a path that we would never have found without you. Our lives have been forever changed because of you and we will be forever grateful."

Cathryn's star power and passion for cheetahs has reached far and wide. Broadway actress and singer Judy McLane recalls the impact Cathryn had on her life. "I met Cathryn backstage after performing on Broadway with the Cincinnati Symphony Orchestra in 2002. When we met, I expressed that I'd love to do whatever I could to help the plight of the cheetah. Cathryn said to me, 'When you hear that purr and look into the eyes of a cheetah, you'll never be the same.' She was right. I was forever changed. Later that year I joined Cathryn on a trip to Africa—it was the trip of a lifetime. When we returned, I took part in fundraising events as an Angel of Music. I was starring in *Mamma Mia!* on Broadway and would fly to Cincinnati on my day off to sing with other performers. I'll never forget the feeling of singing to Tommy (one of the cheetahs) onstage in front of hundreds of people and being in the presence of such magical animals. I'm forever grateful to Cathryn for the life-changing experiences."

Awards and Recognition for a Lifetime of Dedication to the Cheetah

And now...drumroll...here are the official awards and accolades, tied together in a 40-year run of public love for Cathryn Hosea Hilker.

1981 • Woman of the Year • *The Cincinnati Enquirer* [98]

The headline used by the *Cincinnati Enquirer* to describe Cathryn was simple: "Friend of Animals." Her description as a Woman of the Year was anything but simple.

"As outreach director and coordinator of the Frisch's Discovery Center at the Zoo, Mrs. Hilker organizes a program that takes nature speakers and animals into local schools five days a week for 36 weeks a year. During the summer, Mrs. Hilker and the Zoo educators gear up rather than down. The program has been so successful that several zoos across the nation have reproduced it. This year, the Discovery Center won the top education award from the American Association of Zoological Parks and Aquariums."

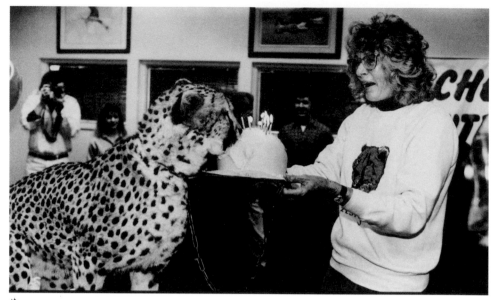

🐾 Happy Birthday Angel!

Cathryn's approach was high engagement: "We kept the groups small so every kid could touch the animals." In Cathryn's view, the Zoo was a natural place for her to devote her time: "I always raised little orphan animals and rode horses."[99]

With customary humility, Cathryn was surprised but thrilled to get the *Enquirer* award. "I always assumed the award went to professional women, women who discovered brain cures or transplanted things. All I do is work at the Zoo. But I'm happy because these programs have touched so many children in so many ways."

1998 • Norma Martin Goodall Distinguished Alumna Award • Seven Hills School [100]

"In 1998, Cathryn was awarded the Goodall Distinguished Alumna Award, given as the highest honor Seven Hills bestows on a graduate who has achieved distinction in a public or private career or activity bettering the lives of others. As Head Trainer for the Cat Ambassador Program at the Cincinnati Zoo & Botanical Garden, Cathryn Hilker had brought her message of wildlife conservation and cheetah preservation to countless children and adults in her school outreach programs, her summer shows at the Zoo, and her appearances on national TV programs. After the death of Angel the cheetah, Cathryn established The Angel Fund which has been responsible for the creation of a cheetah breeding facility at the Zoo's Loveland, Ohio, farm and a preserve in Namibia which is the headquarters of the international Cheetah Conservation Fund.

When Head of School Debbie Reed asked Cathryn Hilker what to say about her, Cathryn said 'Tell them I have helped the cheetah.' Now there is an understatement! Cathryn has single-handedly taken on the task of educating hundreds of school children, their families, and their teachers about these creatures. No one could love more or have done more for us or for 'God's creatures' than Cathryn Hilker."

Miss Hosea at Hillsdale School (1965)

2000 • Wildlife Conservation Award shared with Dr. Laurie Marker • Cincinnati Zoo & Botanical Garden

Each year, the Cincinnati Zoo invites several of the world's leading conservationists to participate in the Barrows Conservation Lecture Series[101] and presents a Wildlife Conservation Award to one of the speakers. The list of

Cathryn Hilker and Dr. Laurie Marker with Angel and Lexi

internationally known conservationists who have been honored with this award is impressive. Beginning with the first recipient in 1993, Jane Goodall, and including the award shared in 2000 by Cathryn Hilker and Dr. Laurie Marker, the Zoo has recognized many outstanding conservationists of our time. Hilker and Marker were then, and now, among the most widely recognized experts on cheetah conservation in the world.

At the time that Cathryn and Dr. Marker were honored with the Zoo's conservation award, Thane Maynard was the Zoo's Director of Education. He explains why the Zoo decided to give the conservation award to Cathryn, and what happened when she was surprised with the award during the event:

"Cathryn and Hege Hilker literally bought the initial 28,000-acre farm in Namibia for the Cheetah Conservation Fund in two parcels during 1995–96. Cathryn didn't know about the Zoo's award ahead of time. Keep in mind she was 69 at the time. So I get up to the podium and announce Cathryn's name as the recipient. Of course, she wasn't prepared with any remarks because she was taken aback. She comes to the podium, standing in front of the microphone in a room of 200 people, holding the award in her hands. Then she says, 'Well, all I can say is it was my husband's money. Thank you.' And then she sat down."

2004 • Honorary Doctor of Science • University of Cincinnati

"Even though Cathryn Hilker was born, raised, and still resides in the Cincinnati area, she has traveled the world in her endeavors as a 'Champion of Wildlife.' She is an internationally recognized and revered conservationist, a sought-after speaker and world-class educator. Her life-time devotion to wildlife in general, and to the survival of the African cheetah in particular, has resulted in permanent preservation of this endangered and beautiful species.

Cathryn is a graduate of the University of Cincinnati, having received her degree in cultural anthropology a half-century ago. She

Dr. Nancy L. Zimpher and Cathryn (2004)

has used her knowledge as a teacher and educator, and even though she is recognized world-wide for her conservation efforts with cheetahs, she is almost as well-known for her educational endeavors. Her contributions to the Cincinnati Zoo are legendary.

Cathryn Hilker is truly a person who has made a difference. Through her zeal and persistence, and unflagging devotion to the preservation of wildlife, the cheetah is no longer headed toward extinction."[102]

Dr. Nancy L. Zimpher, then-president of the University of Cincinnati, conferred Cathryn's honorary degree with these words of praise:[103]

In a world beset by problems largely spawned by indifference, a dedicated passion is the antidote. From the time you carried forth your diploma from this institution, you have dedicated yourself to teaching, and return today as one of the world's outstanding educators. Over the years you have exhibited a remarkable clarity of vision and the singular ability to change lives by sharing knowledge. Importantly, you have matched these educational skills with the capacity for effective action leading to world-wide influence. Your zeal and devotion to the preservation of wildlife and the environment carries promise of a better future for us all.

The more things change, the more they stay the same. Sixteen years later, Dr. Zimpher says "to this day, it is fair to say, to know Cathryn Hilker is to live vicariously in the world of the wilds and at the same time in the world of the possible. My role model!"

2007 • President's Award • Public Relations Society of America, Cincinnati Chapter

The Public Relations Society of America (PRSA) is an association representing more than 30,000 professional and student members. The Cincinnati Chapter of PRSA, one of 110 such groups in the country, gives a president's award each year to honor a Cincinnatian who does not work in the public relations profession, but who uses PR essentials—strategy, storytelling, and brand building—to bring positive awareness of and reputation to the City of

🐾 Cathryn at the Wildlife Theatre

Cincinnati. Cathryn was congratulated for her cheetah conservation ambassador work for the Cincinnati Zoo and internationally.

2010 • Great Living Cincinnatian • Cincinnati USA Regional Chamber

"It's not an exaggeration to say that Cathryn Hilker is responsible for starting a movement: saving the cheetah from extinction."[104]

Since 1967, the Cincinnati USA Regional Chamber has annually honored a small group of people who have led a life of achievement in business and community service. In 2010, Cathryn shared that honor with Lee Ault Carter, a philanthropist and civic leader; Richard T. Farmer, CEO of the Cintas Corp and founder of the Farmer Family Foundation; and the Rev. Damon Lynch, Jr., a pastor and civil rights leader.

They joined a stellar legion of 118 people previously honored by the Chamber. According to the Chamber's then-CEO Ellen van der Horst, "The class of 2010 is characterized by the traits that drove them to succeed—passion and intense dedication. Their collective impact has been felt not only locally, but nationally and throughout the world."[105]

In his nomination letter to the Chamber, Thane Maynard highlighted compelling reasons for naming Cathryn a Great Living Cincinnatian.[106] "For

🐾 Great Living Cincinnatians (L-R) Lee Carter, Cathryn Hilker, Dick Farmer, and Rev. Damon Lynch, Jr. (2010)

more than 40 years Cathryn has led the charge both at the Cincinnati Zoo and around the world for wildlife and conservation education. In the early 1970s she was one of the founders of the Zoo's Education Department which is today the largest and most significant Zoo education program in the world. She founded the Zoo's Cat Ambassador Program, and she and her cats have helped inspire two generations of Cincinnati students, appearing before more than 1 million children at area schools since 1980. Cathryn has had a global impact on cheetah conservation throughout sub-Saharan Africa. Cathryn Hilker's seminal work has been highly influential, leading the way for many American zoos today to be involved with wildlife in native habitats. I know her as both beloved to the Cincinnati community and a Great Living Cincinnatian."

2014 • Distinguished Alumna Award • University of Cincinnati[107]
"The William Howard Taft Medal for Notable Achievement is given to an alumnus of the University of Cincinnati (UC) based solely on achievements in the recipient's field. Cathryn graduated from UC in 1954 with an Arts & Sciences degree in cultural anthropology, and in 2004 received an honorary Doctor of Science.

UC President Santa Ono and Cathryn (2014)

It's a terrible irony that the fastest creatures on earth were collectively facing a slow death in the changing African environment where they once had thrived. But recent years have seen a reversal of fortune for wild cheetahs as their populations have stabilized. The change can be traced to Cincinnati and the efforts of Cathryn Hilker of the Cincinnati Zoo & Botanical Garden.

After receiving her UC degree in Cultural Anthropology, Hilker set out on a two-month adventure. She had no way of knowing her African expedition would be a precursor to a career dedicated to educating the public about wild animals in general and the cheetah in particular —or that she would play a pivotal role in helping save this cat in the wild.

The Angel Fund and Hilker's tireless efforts also positioned the Cincinnati Zoo as one of the world's premier cheetah breeding centers, and led the zoo to develop its Cheetah Encounter, the first zoo environment in the world where visitors can see cheetahs run at top speed on a daily basis."

2017 • Cheetah Conservation Award • Cheetah Conservation Fund

In anticipation of its 30th anniversary in 2020, the Cheetah Conservation Fund (CCF) decided it was time to begin publicly honoring the people who've made it possible for CCF to claim its reputation as the longest running cheetah conservation program in the world. Cathryn was the first award recipient in 2017.

"Cathryn Hilker is a dear friend and big cat supporter that has been long associated with CCF and its mission of creating a permanent place for cheetahs on Earth," said Dr. Laurie Marker at the public event. "It is an honor to know Cathryn, and I am exceptionally pleased to be giving her this award. She has dedicated a significant portion of her life to sustaining the cheetah and pioneering cat ambassador programs."[108]

Among many accolades, Cathryn was a founding member of the CCF board of directors. She and her husband made it possible to purchase the first

🐾 (L-R) Delane Starliper and Karen Maier, Dr. Laurie Marker, Craig and Anne Maier, Cathryn Hilker, Scott and Dana Maier, Thane Maynard

28,000-acre parcel of land for the CCF bulkhead. Cathryn helped CCF bring 10 cheetahs to zoos in the United States (including two to the Cincinnati Zoo's Cheetah Breeding Facility).

With great fondness, Laurie Marker reflects that "Cathryn and I are both big horseback riders. Every time I would ride with her in Ohio, in the woods around her farm, it was golden light with Fall colors. She was a great horse woman."

🐾 Cathryn and Dr. Laurie Marker in Mason, Ohio

Acknowledgments

Special thanks and much gratitude to the people who set this book project in motion, kept it going smoothly through rounds of interviews and edits, and facilitated Cathryn's engagement in developing the book from start to finish.

Cora Ogle and Nancy Zimpher convinced a reluctant Cathryn that 2020 would be the ideal time to get her story written down, and guided content as stories unfolded. Juli Lowry and Kris Kalnow made sure that Cathryn was ready "with bells on" for interviews and storytelling. Ellen van der Horst lent a critical editorial eye to multiple versions of the manuscript.

Thane Maynard and Christina Anderson gave unbridled access to information about Cathryn's tenure at the Cincinnati Zoo. Other Zoo contributors include Linda Castañeda, Gary Denzler, Reba Dysart, Dave Jenike, Kathleen Stewart Maynard, Ed Maruska, and Alicia Sampson.

So many people contributed resources for the book, including Cathryn's son, Carl Hilker III. Thank you for shining light on Cathryn's amazing life and contributions to cheetah conservation. Long-time friends who provided stories for the book included Dr. Diane Babcock, Cathy Jacob, Marian Liebold, Lily Maynard, Barbara McCulloh, and Judy McLane.

Representing institutions key to Cathryn's story, thank you to Chris Garten and Sarah Lautar, Seven Hills School; Mary Paris, Mary Lewis, and Christopher Hildreth, The Jane Goodall Institute; Marianne Kunnen-Jones, the University of Cincinnati; Gary Hang Lee, principal with CLR Design; Carolyn McCoy, Greater Cincinnati Foundation; and Dr. Laurie Marker, Cheetah Conservation Fund.

And a very special thanks to the professional photographers whose beautiful work is featured in the book—Amanda Cawdrey, Cassandre Crawford, Stuart Fabe, Paul Silvers, and W. F. Schildman.

Photo Index

Unless otherwise credited, all photographs are from Cathryn Hilker's personal collection or the Cincinnati Zoo & Botanical Garden.

Endnotes

Chapter 1

1. Members of the Silent Generation were born between 1925 and 1945, so called because they were raised during a period of war and economic depression.
2. *Ancestry.com* and the 1940 U.S. Census.
3. The now-defunct H & FH Hosea Company founded by Cathryn's father is not related to the Hosea Project Movers company, an industrial relocation expert headquartered in Covington, Kentucky, owned by David S. and D. Todd Hosea.
4. Cathryn Hilker's early life stories written in 2012.
5. Ibid.

Chapter 2

6. *e-yearbook.com*. University of Colorado, "Coloradan Yearbook" 1951 and 1952.
7. After World War II, the U.S. Air Force and Navy maintained troops on the island of Guam, which is strategically situated in the North Pacific Ocean. Anderson Air Force Base, established in 1944, is to this day the most important base for the Asia-Pacific region. Source: "USAF Heritage 1945-2020."
8. Unless otherwise noted, the story of Cathryn's 1957 trip to Africa is drawn from interviews, narration of Cathryn's 16 mm film, and a tale about the encounter which Cathryn wrote in 2002.
9. *Dairy Goat Journal*, Selected 1956 and 1957 Editions. "The Gift of Goat Milk," Nov/Dec 2017. (*countrysidenetwork.com*)
10. "Jungle—What's That?" *Cincinnati Enquirer*, Aug. 7, 1960, p. 45.
11. Today Leopoldville is called Kinshasa. It is the capital city of the Democratic Republic of the Congo.
12. David Ehrlinger, *The Cincinnati Zoo and Botanical Garden From Past to Present* (Cincinnati Zoo & Botanical Garden: 1993), p. 82.
13. "City Zoo to Get New Gorilla As Gift From Dr. Schweitzer." *Cincinnati Enquirer*, June 7, 1957, p. 5.
14. "Gorilla is Donated to Zoo by Bernard." *Cincinnati Enquirer*, July 30, 1957, p.5.
15. Cathryn attended what was most likely one of the final celebrations of the Watusi tribe in the area that became Burundi in 1962 after independence from Belgium.
16. A 1989 article in the *Cincinnati Enquirer* reports Dr. Bernard saying that he broke his back when he fell off the truck while in Africa. Perhaps this was the partial reason for his sudden departure?
17. Dale Peterson, *Jane Goodall: The Woman who Redefined Man* (New York: Houghton Mifflin Company, 2006), pp. 150-55, pp. 157-58, and p. 164.
18. Olduvai Gorge in Tanzania is one of the world's most important paleoanthropological sites.
19. Dr. Leakey advised each of the young women who wanted to work for him in Africa to have her appendix removed, including Dian Fossey who conducted gorilla studies. The purpose was to prevent the possibility of a burst appendix in a remote area with no hospital access—a tragedy that had happened previously.

20. libapps.libraries.uc.edu/exhibits/barbour/biography.

21. geosociety.org/documents/gsa/memorials/v09/Barbour-GB.pdf.

22. *Cincinnati Enquirer,* "Jungle—What's That?"

23. Excerpts from janegoodall.org/our-story/about-jane/

24. Jane Goodall with Thane Maynard and Gail Hudson, *Hope for Animals and Their World: How Endangered Species Are Being Rescued From The Brink* (New York: Grand Central Publishing, 2009), pp. xv-xvii.

Chapter 3

25. Bill Hoff was Cincinnati Zoo Director from July 1961 through November 1967.

26. Cathryn is quick to point out that raising a young tiger at home would not be permitted today under strict modern zoo safety policy and practice. "Toughy the Tiger" is a unique moment-in-time story.

27. Toughy the Tiger apparently was the genesis of Cathryn's lifetime habit of using duct tape to solve most leakage problems.

28. Founded initially as "Miss Doherty's School," a private college preparatory high school, a 1974 merger with the Hillsdale-Lotspeich School was renamed The Seven Hills School.

29. legacy.com obituary, February 20, 2016.

30. Ibid.

31. *Dayton Daily News*, September 24, 2014.

32. Barbara Clark, "Meet Hooty: Family Finds Raising Horned Owl Fabulous," *The Western Star*, September 6, 1978.

33. *Dayton Daily News.*

34. See Chapter 5 for more about the Hilkers' relationship with the Cheetah Conservation Fund.

35. Jane Durrell; photos by David Steinbrunner, "Where the Wild Things Are," *Cincinnati Magazine*, September 1999, pp. 70-75 and 112-113.

Chapter 4

36. The Cincinnati Zoo was founded in 1873 by Andrew Erkenbrecker, a German immigrant known for his vision, enthusiasm, and determination. It was initially called the Cincinnati Zoological garden. It opened to the public on September 18, 1874, the second zoo in the United States (after Philadelphia, 14 months earlier). In 1987, the zoo's name was officially changed to the Cincinnati Zoo & Botanical Garden.

37. Ed Maruska joined the Zoo as curator in 1962 and was named Zoo director in 1968.

38. animals24-7.org/2014/05/14/al-oeming-88-ran-alberta-game-farm-for-40-years/

39. edmontonjournal.com/news/local-news/may-14-1957-cheetah-frightens-west-end-residents

40. *Cincinnati Enquirer*, October 1, 1972, p. 148.

41. Oliver M. Gale. "The Cincinnati Zoo: 100 Years of Trial and Triumph." Undated.

42. *Zoomin'* Spring 1987, p. 34.

43. David Ehrlinger, *Zoo From Past to Present.*

44. Oliver M Gale.

45. Coleen Armstrong, "Thane Maynard's Window on the Wild," *Cincinnati Magazine*, May 1997, p. 33.

46. *Zoomin'* Spring 1987, p. 34.

47. David Ehrlinger, *Zoo From Past to Present*, p. 108.

48. Ibid.

49. References for Ed Maruska's story include a personal interview on October 1, 2020; David Erlinger's book on the history of the Cincinnati Zoo; and a 2017 interview with Ed published on zoophoria.net. Quotes are taken from these sources.

50. Edward J. Maruska. "Preserving the Past for Future Generations," Zoo & Aquarium Video Archives, 2020.

51. Coleen Armstrong, pp. 35 & 37.

52. Ibid.

53. Jenny Wohlfarth, "Zookeeper's Tale," *Cincinnati Magazine*, March 1, 2013.

54. The Explorers Club is a US-based international society that promotes scientific exploration and field study. A photojournalist for *National Geographic*, Mike Fay was honored for his 465-day expedition on foot across 2,000 miles across the Congo basin of Africa. During his acceptance speech, Mike "gave" the award to Cathryn, acknowledging the importance of her cheetah conservation work in Namibia, describing what individuals can do for conservation when they think about exploring in an entirely different way.

55. Craig and Karen Maier interview on August 14, 2020.

56. Interviews with Kris Kalnow on 8/7/2020 and 9/16/2020 (condensed).

57. Even today, the Echo offers a daily codfish sandwich, but only on Fridays the sandwich is made from halibut—a special treat!

58. Oliver M. Gale.

59. Cheetah Conservation Fund Newsletter, "Namibia's Ambassador Meets Cheetah Ambassador." No. 18, Summer 2002.

60. Ibid.

61. "Charmed by Charles," *Broward Sun-Sentinal.* March 7, 1988.

Chapter 5

62. Cincinnati Zoo. "Cheetah: The Story of An Endangered Species."

63. "Cheetahs on the Edge," *National Geographic*, November 2012, p. 112.

64. Cheetah Conservation Fund (CCF) and other sources.

65. CCF, "Cheetah Survival on Namibian Farmlands," 1996.

66. *National Geographic*, pp 113-114.

67. Ibid.

68. *National Geographic*, p. 118.

69. David Ehrlinger, *Zoo From Past to Present*, p. 94.

70. Angel's story is the focus of Chapter 6.

71. Ibid.

72. Greg Hanson, *Wildlife Explorer*, 1998, p. 16.

73. Joy Kraft, *Images of America,* (Mt. Pleasant, SC: Arcadia Publishing, 2010), p. 127.

74. CREW. "Saving Species with Science" undated.

75. In addition to CCF, there are several other international organizations that focus on endangered wildlife, including cheetahs in Africa and Asia. But CCF in Namibia, and Cheetah Outreach in South Africa, are the only organizations devoted to cheetah conservation in the wild where cheetahs are concentrated today.

76. wildlifesafari.net/cheetahs/

77. cheetah.org/about/who-we-are/ccf-mission/

78. *Dayton Daily News*, September 24, 2014.

79. Ibid.

80. *Zoo Wildlife Explorer*, September 1996, p. 9.

81. cheetah.co.za/co_staff

82. *Zoo Wildlife Explorer*, p. 16.

Chapter 6

83. Cathryn Hosea Hilker, *A Cheetah Named Angel*, (A Cincinnati Zoo Publication, Franklin Watts Publishing, 1992).

84. *Zoomin'* Spring 1987, p. 32.

85. Jimmy Stewart and Betty White were co-chairs of Zoofari in 1983.

86. Royalties from sales of Cathryn's biography will help to replenish and reactivate The Angel Fund's mission.

87. Cathryn Hilker's personal journal, February 1, 2007.

Chapter 7

88. Stephanie Pappas, *Life Science Contributor*, August 2, 2012.

89. Ibid.

90. Camila Domonoske, "Sarah The Cheetah, World's Fastest Land Animal, Dies At 15." NPR, January 22, 2016.

91. Cincinnati Zoo blog, 2016.

92. Ibid.

Chapter 8

93. Sadly, none of these photos survived the passing of time in Cathryn's trunk!

94. Mokoro is a hand-made dug-out canoe commonly used in the Okavango Delta and throughout Botswana. It is propelled through the shallow waters of the delta or the river by standing in the stern and pushing with a pole. The Cincinnati Zoo has a mokoro canoe on display for viewing by guests.

95. This story is taken from an interview with Lily Maynard on September 3, 2020.

Chapter 9

96. alumni.uc.edu/events/alumni-celebration/alumni-celebration-past-recipients/2014-award-recipients

97. Cindy Starr, "Giving Cheetahs a Place to Roam," *Deseret News*, March 30, 1997.

98. *Cincinnati Enquirer*, January 31, 1982, p. 75.

99. Ibid.

100. "1998 Goodall Distinguished Alumna/us Awards honor Louise Wachman Spiegel ('42) and Cathryn Hosea Hilker ('49)." Seven Hills program for the Summer 1998 Class Reunion, April 24, 1998.

101. The lecture series was endowed by Winnie Barrows, a Cincinnati Zoo board member and supporter.

102. University of Cincinnati. "Cheetahs' 'Angel' Hilker Honored by UC." June 8, 2004.

103. University of Cincinnati, 2004.

104. Great Living Cincinnatians video presentation for Cathryn Hilker, February 24, 2011.

105. *Cincinnati Enquirer*, February 26, 2010, p. 19.

106. Provided by the Cincinnati Zoo.

107. alumni.uc.edu/events/alumni-celebration/alumni-celebration-past-recipients/2014-award-recipients

108. CCF press release, March 29, 2017.